SILVER
OPPORTUNITY

CASE STUDIES

SILVER
OPPORTUNITY

CASE STUDIES

Experiences with Building Integrated Services
for Older Adults around Primary Health Care

**Edited by Xiaohui Hou,
Jigyasa Sharma, and
Feng Zhao**

WORLD BANK GROUP

Contents

Chapter 6. The Unmet Need: Assessing the Demand for and Supply of Home-Based Support for Older Adults with Disabilities in European Countries and Comparators   93

Yuting Qian, Shanquan Chen, Xiaohui Hou, Zhuoer Lin, Zexuan Yu,
Mengxiao Wang, and Xi Chen

Chapter 7. Conclusions and Policy Directions   113

Jigyasa Sharma, Xiaohui Hou, Feng Zhao, and Alexander Irwin

Boxes

Figures

Map

Tables

Foreword

Population aging is a development triumph, thanks to country efforts to improve health outcomes that have resulted in rising life expectancy and plunging fertility rates. The unprecedented and rapid aging of the global population is one of the most consequential transformations of the twenty-first century. This demographic transition will explode by mid-century, interacting with other trends and shaping the future of our planet. By 2050, the population ages 60 and older is expected to reach 2.1 billion, more than double the number in 2017.

Older adults have much to contribute to society. They are not only skilled volunteers and informal family caregivers—they also add value to economies through paid employment, and their share of the workforce is growing. It is important to point out that population aging is not restricted to high-income countries. It exists across regions and, over the next decade, will also profoundly affect youthful Sub-Saharan Africa.

But warning signs abound. Most health care systems are not prepared to meet the needs of the growing numbers of older people, especially the growing burden of noncommunicable diseases (NCDs) and chronic conditions that require prolonged medical and social care.

Investing in and improving the health—and, therefore, the productivity—of this swelling population will pay dividends not only for older people and their families but also for economies.

However, if governments do not prepare for this demographic surge and create more resilient health systems that respond to the needs of seniors, the dividends from population aging will turn into losses for individuals and countries.

The 2023 publication *Silver Opportunity: Building Integrated Services for Older Adults around Primary Health Care* made the case that the key to success is anchoring person-centered integrated services for older adults in primary health care.

This new 2024 publication, *Silver Opportunity Case Studies: Experiences with Building Integrated Services for Older Adults around Primary Health Care*, provides evidence and practical tools for countries to strengthen health outcomes for older adults while controlling health system costs. It focuses on promising country experiences with adopting measures to catalyze healthier, longer lives. It also discusses the shortcomings in health systems that impede robust health care for older adults and policy recommendations to overcome these obstacles.

This publication comes at a critical time. The world has just six years left to achieve the ambitious targets of the Sustainable Development Goals, including ensuring healthy lives and well-being for people "at all ages." To fuel progress so that people can age with dignity and lead more productive, healthy, and meaningful lives, the United Nations has declared the 2020s to be the Decade of Healthy Aging.

By strengthening health systems, governments can speed progress toward universal health coverage (UHC). Countries are encouraged to orient their UHC investments toward groups most at risk of poorer health outcomes—and with the rising NCD burden, older adults certainly qualify.

We have precious little time left to create resilient health systems that can address the unique needs of this burgeoning population. If we act now, we can build healthier, more prosperous societies that will benefit—and benefit from—older people and their families, communities, and countries.

Juan Pablo Uribe
Global Director, Health, Nutrition, and Population Global Practice
The World Bank

Acknowledgments

This report was led by Xiaohui Hou (senior economist) and Jigyasa Sharma (economist). The work was undertaken under the supervision and guidance of Monique Vledder (practice manager, Global Engagement, Health, Nutrition, and Population Global Practice), Feng Zhao (practice manager, South Asia Region, Health, Nutrition, and Population Global Practice), and Jumana Qamruddin (team lead, Service Delivery, Health, Nutrition, and Population Global Practice). David Wilson (program director, Global Engagement, Health, Nutrition, and Population Global Practice) and Juan Pablo Uribe (global director, Health, Nutrition, and Population Global Practice) provided additional overall guidance. Mickey Chopra, Victoria Fan, and Sameera M. Al Tuwaijri provided critical comments as peer reviewers. Alexander Irwin, Louise Stoddard, and Karen Schneider provided writing and editorial support. Jocelyn Haye and Marize de Fatima Santos provided administrative support. Naoko Ohno (senior operations officer) and Kyoko Tokuda (operations officer) provided trust fund administration guidance and support.

The volume's core chapters draw from the following policy notes:

Time to Focus on Healthy Aging Challenges, Opportunities, and Recommendations for Bangladesh

Khaleda Islam, Seemi Qaiser, Kathryn Andrews, Jigyasa Sharma, Xiaohui Hou, Bushra Binte Alam, and Atia Hossain

Integrated People-Centered Care for an Aging Population: Colombia Case Study

Lenis Urquijo, Jose Valderrama, Juan Arango, and Juan Pablo Toro

Meeting the Growing Health Needs of an Older Population: The Case of Mongolia

Tumurbat Byamba, Evlegsuren Ser-Od, Khishgee Majigzav, Enkhjargal Altangerel, Tsolmongerel Tsilaajav, Naranzul Nyamsuren, Unurmaa Enebish, Nandintsetseg Tsoggerel, Tsogzolmaa Khurelerdene, Pagma Genden, Kate Mandeville, Vikram Rajan, and Xiaohui Hou

Integrated People-Centered Care for an Aging Population: A Case Study of the UAE

Omniyat M. Al Hajeri, Sameh El-Saharty, Hamed A. Al Hashemi, Sara Barada, Arwa Al-Modwahi, and Anderson Stanciole

Long-Term Care for Aging Populations in Africa: Current Landscape, Key Challenges, and Policy Considerations

Zhanlian Feng, Natalie Mulmule, Xiaohui Hou, and Jigyasa Sharma

The Unmet Need: Assessing the Demand for and Supply of Home-Based Support for Older Adults with Disabilities

Yuting Qian, Shanquan Chen, Xiaohui Hou, Zhuoer Lin, Zexuan Yu, Mengxiao Wang, and Xi Chen

The policy papers can be found at https://documents.worldbank.org/en /publication/documents-reports/documentlist?colti=%22silver%20opportunity %20case%20study%20series%22&srt=docdt&order=desc.

We are grateful to the Japan Policy and Human Resources Development Fund (PHRD) Trust Fund for its support of this report.

About the Editors

Xiaohui Hou is a senior economist in the World Bank's Health, Nutrition, and Population Global Practice. She has more than 15 years of experience in development and specializes in health financing, service delivery, and health systems strengthening. Throughout her career, she has led policy dialogues, lending operations, flagship analytical projects, and program development in various countries across Africa, East Asia and the Pacific, Eastern Europe, and South Asia. Her work has been published in books and peer-reviewed journals in the field of economics and health. Recently, she undertook an external services opportunity as the Deputy Head of the Subregional Office for East and North-East Asia in the United Nations Economic and Social Commission for Asia and the Pacific. She has served as a visiting scholar at several universities. She holds a PhD in health services and policy analysis and a master's degree in economics from the University of California, Berkeley; a master's degree in health policy and administration from Washington State University; and a bachelor's degree in biochemistry and molecular biology from Beijing University.

Jigyasa Sharma is a health economist in the World Bank's Health, Nutrition, and Population Global Practice. She joined the World Bank in September 2019 in the Office of the Chief Economist for Human Development. Her areas of expertise include health systems strengthening and measurement of health system quality and primary care performance. A population health and health system researcher, she has coauthored dozens of journal articles and reports on health system quality and measurement of quality of care, contributed to the Lancet Global Health Commission for High Quality Health Systems, and worked as a consultant for the Department of Reproductive Health and Research at the World Health Organization. She holds an ScD degree in global health and population from Harvard University and an MSc in epidemiology and biostatistics from McGill University.

Feng Zhao serves as the World Bank's South Asia practice manager in the Health, Nutrition, and Population Global Practice. He has more than 20 years of experience in public health, medicine, economics, and demography at the global, regional, and country levels. Previously, he oversaw the World Bank's Global Health Engagement program and led the COVID-19 (coronavirus) health response program as the manager for Global Health Engagement. He has served in different positions at the World Bank, including program leader for the human development programs for Belarus, Moldova, and Ukraine and task manager for a number of African countries. From August 2009 to July 2011, he was based in the World Bank's Ethiopia country office and served as chair of the Health Partner Group in Ethiopia. He was health manager at the African Development Bank, responsible for health operations in 54 African countries from 2011 to 2014. He serves as a faculty member at a number of universities, including the Harvard Finance Minister Executive Leadership Program. He holds a PhD in population and health economics from Johns Hopkins University; an MPH from the University of California, Berkeley; and a medical degree from China.

Abbreviations

ADL	activity of daily living
AU	African Union
CI	confidence interval
EU	European Union
FHC	family health center
FIRE	financing, innovation, regulation, and evaluation
GDP	gross domestic product
HIV/AIDS	human immunodeficiency virus/acquired immunodeficiency syndrome
IADL	instrumental activity of daily living
ICOPE	Integrated Care for Older People
LTC	long-term care
M&E	monitoring and evaluation
MIPAA	Madrid International Plan of Action on Aging
NCD	noncommunicable disease
NCDC	Noncommunicable Disease Control Programme
ONEV	National Observatory on Aging and Old Age
PHC	primary health care
SABE	Health, Wellness, and Aging survey
SDG	Sustainable Development Goal
SHC	*soum* health center
STEP	STEPwise approach to noncommunicable disease risk factor surveillance
UHC	universal health coverage
WHO	World Health Organization

Building Integrated Services for Older Adults around Primary Health Care: Challenges and Opportunities in Countries

Jigyasa Sharma, Xiaohui Hou, Feng Zhao, and Alexander Irwin

Introduction

A child born in most countries today will almost certainly live longer than his or her parents—a development triumph enabled by countries' progress in health care and ability to meet essential needs. As people live longer, the number of older adults in all societies is rising. By 2050, the global population ages 60 and older will have reached 2.1 billion—double the 2017 figure of 962 million (WHO 2022). This trend will hold not only in countries that already have large populations of older adults, including many countries in East Asia, Europe, and North America, but also in countries with younger populations, like most of Sub-Saharan Africa. In Malawi, Rwanda, Uganda, and Zimbabwe, for example, the number of people ages 60 and older is expected to quadruple by 2050, among the fastest rates of increase in older-adult populations in the world (UN DESA 2022).

Global aging is not just a future projection; it is the present reality. Longer lives open new dimensions of independence and opportunity but also fresh challenges for individuals, households, economies, and governments. Rising populations of older adults demand policy innovations across every domain of governance, from labor markets to health care, social security, housing, transport, technology, and the climate change response. Rapid action to adapt to demographic shifts will bring health and economic rewards for all countries, including those whose populations are still young. Delays in response will carry high opportunity costs (HLI, forthcoming; NAM 2022). For all these reasons, United Nations and World Health Organization member states have designated 2021 to 2030 as a decade of urgent shared action to advance healthy aging through a multisectoral agenda aligned with the Sustainable Development Goals.[1]

A Window of Opportunity to Transform Care Systems

This volume, the second in the World Bank's *Silver Opportunity* collection, shows how some countries are taking steps to enable healthier longer lives for their people by making changes in their health systems. Health care is only a part of the solution to improve well-being among older adults and potentiate their economic and social contributions. Yet health systems are a key part of the policy picture as populations age, both because these systems provide crucial services and because they can impose substantial costs on households and public budgets. The health and economic "double shock" of the COVID-19 pandemic (Kurowski et al. 2021, 2022) has brought home to all countries the importance of having a resilient health system prepared to protect older adults and other vulnerable groups during emergencies, while continuing to deliver quality core health services for all (World Bank 2022).

Rising older-adult populations have resulted in higher demand for health care, particularly for chronic conditions and multiple morbidity, placing countries' health budgets under increasing strain. Simultaneously, population aging poses new challenges for social protection models, labor markets, and economic growth, threatening countries' fiscal balance (HLI, forthcoming; Scott 2021). New approaches are required in the organization, financing, and delivery of health services if health systems are to respond to the needs of aging populations while controlling costs. As they confront these challenges, health systems today are venturing into uncharted territory.

As the work presented in this volume shows, this challenge is also an opportunity to make systems perform more efficiently and yield better outcomes for people of all ages. Current demographic transformations pose important questions about how society as a whole should adapt and distribute its resources to improve the life cycle of the entire population. The changing age distribution of populations therefore presents a window of opportunity to review the shortcomings of existing care systems and fundamentally rethink their design. In health care, countries have a chance to improve efficiency and inclusivity through innovation as they advance toward universal health care. By restructuring policies and programs to meet the needs of older citizens, countries can create systems that work better for all their people. In so doing, they can lay a foundation to reap the full societal and economic benefits of achieving healthier longer lives.

Vast Productive Potential and Diverse Needs

Older adults make high-value contributions to their families, communities, and national economies, and older people have the potential to add still greater value in the future. Recent studies have shown that older adults contribute substantially to national economies through paid work and that their engagement in paid employment is expanding. From 2009 to 2019, growth in employment among people ages 65 years or older accounted for 16 percent to 30 percent of total employment growth in France, Germany, the United Kingdom, and the United States and for as much as 75 percent in Japan (Scott 2021). By improving older adults' health and productivity, countries can reap large economic rewards. A one-year increase in life expectancy achieved through healthier aging would be worth US$38 trillion in the United States alone (Horton 2022). Estimates for the United Kingdom suggest that a one-year extension of older people's healthy working life would increase the country's gross domestic product by around 1 percent (Scott 2021).

Older people's contributions extend far beyond the work they do for pay. Older adults are repositories of social capital, custodians of traditional knowledge, skilled volunteers, and formal and informal caregivers within families and communities. Recent studies have shown that older adults' "productive nonmarket activities," including family care and volunteer work, represent a substantial share of their contribution to value creation in societies (Bloom et al. 2020b).[2] In the United States, on average, adults over age 60 contribute the equivalent of US$20,511 per older adult per year to their communities and households through productive nonmarket activities (Bloom et al. 2020a). This more complete characterization of older people's societal role is vital to broadening the narrative around aging and to incentivizing policy shifts that protect the fundamental rights of older adults and promote inclusivity.

A key consideration for policy is the diversity of older-adult populations. "Older people" are not a homogeneous group. To begin with, important age-related differences exist within this broad age group. The physiological functionality and care needs of typical 60-year-olds differ from those of typical 80-year-olds. Equally important, gender and other cultural norms, societal values, national policy frameworks, and individual preferences introduce or reinforce differences that require flexible, context-specific policy and delivery solutions.

Diversity among older people reflects personal choices but also socioeconomic and health inequalities that are driven by structural factors and that accumulate through people's lifetimes (CSDH 2008; UN DESA 2023; WHO, forthcoming). Inequalities in both healthy and overall life expectancy are increasing in many settings today, both between and within countries (Scott 2021). Past public health initiatives successfully reduced health inequalities for people in childhood and middle age; now the same effort is needed for people in their older years (HLI, forthcoming; O'Keefe and Haldane 2023; Scott 2021). Flexible and adaptable policy solutions tailored to country contexts will be crucial to achieving these aims. Robust approaches will leverage innovation informed by older adults' priorities and preferences. The studies in this volume document solutions that some countries are testing to help people to flourish in their diversity through every stage of life.

The remainder of this overview is structured as follows. The next section outlines the book's conceptual foundations, intended audience, and specific contributions. It relates this publication to *Silver Opportunity* (Hou, Sharma, and Zhao 2023) and other work in the field of healthy longevity and older-adult care. Subsequent sections discuss limitations of the research and summarize key findings from the individual case studies. A final section describes how the rest of the volume is organized.

The *Silver Opportunity* Agenda

Building Integrated Older-Adult Services around Primary Health Care

The publications in the World Bank's *Silver Opportunity* collection aim to provide evidence and practical tools that countries can use to strengthen health outcomes for older adults while controlling health system costs. The collection makes the case that the key to success is anchoring person-centered integrated services for older adults in primary health care (PHC).

The collection speaks in the first instance to national policy makers in health and finance, their advisers, and the system managers and implementers responsible for making care systems work on the ground. It also addresses other stakeholders who shape solutions for healthy and productive aging, including multilateral and bilateral agencies and other institutional development partners; civil society groups, especially organizations of older adults and their advocates; private firms and industry bodies active in the older-adult care space; and the academic research community studying older-adult care systems. Learning and collaboration among all these partners are critical to inform healthy-aging policies and implementation strategies.

Focusing on Care Systems

Silver Opportunity focuses on the health sector. This focus is both a limitation of the work and an important strength. It is a limitation in that many of the key determinants of health and well-being in older adults (as in other populations) lie outside the health sector's direct control and call for a multisectoral approach. This book addresses select sector-spanning issues that have emerged as important through its regional and country case studies. However, it does not propose taking a comprehensive multisectoral approach to older-adult health.

This tightly focused approach allows the *Silver Opportunity* collection to offer granular, practice-oriented knowledge that health sector decision-makers and implementers can use to solve problems. Homing in on a single sector can capture a level of operational detail that broader treatments miss and that is crucial for policy design and effective service delivery on the ground.

This sectoral specificity also enables *Silver Opportunity* to complement groundbreaking recent research on healthier longer lives and policy initiatives that have adopted a multisectoral vision. These initiatives include the World Health Organization's direction-setting work on healthy aging (WHO 2015, 2020), the multifaceted United Nations Decade of Healthy Ageing platform,[3] and landmark research efforts from the World Bank Healthy Longevity Initiative (HLI, forthcoming), Economist Impact and the American Association for Retired Persons (Economist Impact 2022), and the US National Academy of Medicine (NAM 2022).

As a World Bank resource to support action for healthy aging in countries, *Silver Opportunity* is closely aligned with the Healthy Longevity Initiative, whose research products have informed the analysis in this volume. *Silver Opportunity* builds on that effort, opens complementary lines of work, and adds value through its operational focus on the delivery of older-adult care anchored in primary health care. *Silver Opportunity* provides actionable new country-level evidence to illuminate healthy-aging challenges and solutions under real-world conditions. The results open paths for future World Bank collaboration with countries and development partners in operationalizing *Silver Opportunity* evidence and policy recommendations for integrated older-adult care.

Silver Opportunity, Volume 1, and the FIRE Framework

Caring for older adults is a complex challenge. Although each country has its own specific difficulties, most countries also share common issues. To approach problems systematically and facilitate cross-country learning, *Silver Opportunity*, Volume 1, introduces a conceptual framework for PHC-centered integrated older-adult care (figure O.1). The framework highlights four key levers for health system reform to address older adults' care needs: financing, innovation, regulation, and evaluation (FIRE).

Silver Opportunity, Volume 1, builds on prior research and country experience to make the case that primary health care is the best foundation for integrated care systems that can improve older-adult care while containing costs. However, investment shortfalls, system design flaws, and structural barriers inhibit most PHC systems, in their current form, from fully meeting the needs

FIGURE O.1 PHC-Centered Integrated Care for Older Adults: The FIRE Framework

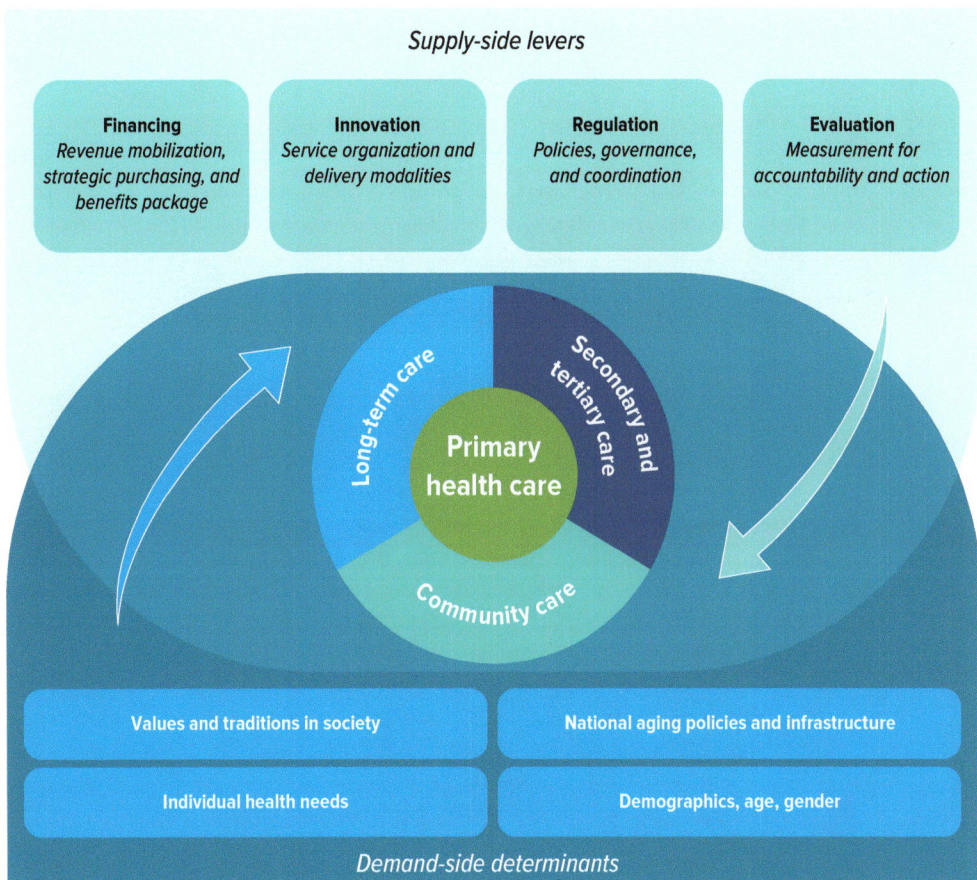

Source: Hou, Sharma, and Zhao 2023.
Note: FIRE = financing, innovation, regulation, and evaluation; PHC= primary health care.

of older adults. To serve older adults better, PHC systems need to deliver quality essential clinical services, while linking seamlessly to secondary and tertiary medical care; long-term care (LTC) networks, including home-based and facility-based options; and community resources that can support older people's health, social connectedness, dignity, and productivity.

Historically, such models of integrated care have proven difficult to achieve, including in high-income settings. However, *Silver Opportunity*, Volume 1, finds that some countries have made notable progress. The volume surveys the global literature and proposed evidence-based principles for reform under the four FIRE pillars. It closes with a case study of Japan's community-based integrated care system for older adults, which confirmed the value of documenting country experience with integrated older-adult care while also highlighting the current shortage of country-level evidence in this important area (JICA, Nakayama, and Hou 2023).

Silver Opportunity, Volume 2: Expanding the Country-Level Evidence Base

The current volume aims to bridge this evidence gap. It examines care for older adults in diverse economic and geographic contexts through country and regional case studies. Each study analyzes local issues related to population aging and care provision for older adults, details policies and interventions in its setting of interest, discusses implementation barriers and solutions, and draws lessons from the country's or region's experience. The volume's overarching goal is to inform policy makers, system managers, health care professionals, and other stakeholders about effective practices in older-adult care and to support future evidence-based policies.

Contribution of the Individual Studies

The country case studies in this book were chosen to reflect broad geographic, economic, demographic, and health system diversity, while facilitating peer learning among countries. Research questions focus on salient local concerns that may also have wider policy resonance. Thus, the Bangladesh study highlights issues that arise in a rapidly aging lower-middle-income country whose health system is oriented toward acute disease care even as the burden of chronic noncommunicable diseases (NCDs) climbs. The study reports on key investment and service-provision gaps affecting older adults but also identifies promising PHC-based initiatives that may be tested further, improved, and scaled to bolster NCD prevention and control in Bangladesh.

Colombia, an upper-middle-income country, has registered impressive health gains in recent years, but stark socioeconomic and health disparities persist, especially affecting older people. The case study analyzes options to improve health and health equity among older Colombians through a PHC-based care model that engages socioeconomic determinants of healthy aging.

Delivering care to older people in rural settings is a challenge in many countries. Mongolia is a lower-middle-income country characterized by a thinly spread nomadic rural population along with rapid growth in its capital city, Ulan Bator. The case study explores how the country's health system can improve access to care and outcomes for older adults, particularly in rural areas, by engaging in targeted collaboration with the social welfare sector and by strengthening programs such as population-based screening for noncommunicable diseases and risk factors in PHC settings.

COVID-19 showed that the convergence of population aging and emerging infectious diseases can overwhelm health systems even in the richest countries. Improving health care access, quality, and outcomes among older people is crucial to achieving health security for all. The case study of the United Arab Emirates looks at how an innovative service delivery model for vulnerable older adults enabled an effective response to COVID-19 in the capital city, Abu Dhabi, yielding lessons for health action that may also improve outcomes in noncrisis times.

The volume's two regional studies reflect broad economic and health system diversity, while highlighting opportunities to learn across contexts. Rising populations of older adults pose complex challenges in Sub-Saharan Africa, where many health systems face severe resource constraints and LTC systems are nascent. The case study of Sub-Saharan Africa looks at how countries across the continent are responding and draws lessons for policy making and implementation. The authors make the case that countries can leverage existing PHC infrastructure to deliver key components of long-term care, such as screening for chronic disease and nursing care. They show the advantages for Africa of mixed LTC systems able to supplement traditional family-based care with quality professionalized services—an approach that also holds promise for other settings.

The volume's final case study documents the need for and access to care among older adults with disabilities in 27 European countries and 4 global comparators, a total of 31 mostly high- and upper-income countries. The study leverages quantitative data analysis to propose entry points for policy to narrow the gaps in care among vulnerable older adults.

Case Study Methods

The case studies adopt various methodologies, described in the individual chapters. Most use qualitative or mixed-methods approaches to data collection and analysis. As noted, the regional study of European countries and comparators was designed explicitly to show how a more quantitative analytic approach can provide actionable insights for older-adult care policy in countries where the necessary data are available.

The country case studies use the four-pillar FIRE framework as a common entry point. Some studies delve deeper into one or two pillars, while others examine all four pillars. For instance, the United Arab Emirates case study highlights the use of innovative digital health technology, while the 31-country comparative study highlights the use of data to understand trends in demand among older adults and to assess whether these demands are being met—an important aspect of the evaluation pillar. This variety of approaches allows for a flexible examination of older-adult care needs and care systems and the unique challenges and opportunities that exist in each setting.

The case studies in this volume are condensed versions of longer policy notes and empirical papers. Readers with a deeper interest in specific settings are invited to refer to the original policy notes or papers and the additional data they contain.[4] The development of these cases was made possible through consultations with local policy makers, health professionals, and other stake-holders. The case studies presented are snapshots of current policy and implementation status. Taking into account the rapid pace of demographic transition, this volume marks the beginning of important work.

Study Limitations

It is important to acknowledge the limitations of this research. These limitations concern the case studies themselves, individually and collectively, as well as the underlying FIRE framework, which the country-level researchers have used as an analytic entry point.

- *Small number of studies.* It is not possible to draw sweeping scientific or policy conclusions based on the small number of regional and country studies included here. Together with the Japan study from *Silver Opportunity*, Volume 1, the case studies in this volume explore country and regional experiences across various geographies, income levels, and political-economy conditions. However, they are far from capturing the full range of country concerns and policy options in older-adult care. Synthesis of findings across the studies is difficult given their methodological diversity. While the country research teams reviewed each other's research questions, plans, and methods and the teams proceeded in broadly consistent ways, each team tailored its methodology to its specific learning goals and national conditions. In presenting and interpreting the results, the aim here is not to formulate broad prescriptions, but to suggest starting points for deliberating policy and implementation in diverse settings through illustrative examples.

- *Data constraints.* All of the national research teams encountered substantial gaps in data and evidence relative to older-adult care provision and outcomes. Most teams consider these data gaps to be a significant constraint to improving health outcomes among older adults in the settings they studied. Nationally or subnationally representative data on older adults' health care needs and preferences, health care use, and spending remain scanty, hampering the ability to generate evidence-driven policy solutions. Research teams call on governments and development partners to recognize data as a priority area for strengthening integrated older-adult care.

- *Cross-sectional study design.* As noted, the country case studies provide synchronic "snapshots" of the state of policy and service delivery for older adults in a given setting at a specified time. With rare exceptions, the studies do not track the results of programs through time, as framing conditions and the interventions themselves evolve.[5] The absence of tracking further limits the normative reach of the policy and implementation lessons drawn.

- *Limited analysis of multisectoral approaches.* Many of the most powerful determinants of older adults' health lie outside the direct control of the health sector and demand multisectoral, whole-of-government, or (ideally) whole-of-society approaches to policy design and delivery (CSDH 2008; Govindaraj and Gopalan 2023; WHO, forthcoming). While acknowledging the critical importance of multisectoral strategies, the *Silver Opportunity* work aims to add value by focusing on issues related to the design and delivery of care, issues that are largely under the direct influence of health policy makers. The analysis engages multisectoral issues and options only in a few cases, most notably around bridging PHC-centered health care delivery and multifaceted long-term care for older adults with disabilities, a concern common across many settings. Opportunities to strengthen older adults' health and well-being through policies related to job markets and income support (notably pensions) are discussed prominently in the Bangladesh and Colombia country cases and in the regional study of Sub-Saharan Africa.

- *Inclusion of only some important forms of country experience.* While the case studies reflect substantial diversity in geography, political economy, country income levels, and health system conditions, many salient forms of country experience are not represented. Notably, these studies have not tried to capture the health system challenges associated with fragility and conflict. Additional studies, curating evidence across multiple sources, are needed to gain a better understanding of the health risks facing older adults in contexts of fragility, conflict, and systemic violence and to identify mitigation strategies.

  The consequences of climate change, food insecurity, water shortages, and global economic turbulence add further layers of complexity to the aging story. For example, large movements of refugees and other migrants between countries have far-reaching fiscal and other implications for health care delivery. More country case studies and implementation science research on the delivery of key services for older adults—including, but not limited to, the prevention, care, and management of chronic diseases—are needed across global regions, especially in low- and middle-income settings (HLI, forthcoming; NCD Countdown 2030 Collaborators 2022).

- *Limitations of the FIRE framework.* The FIRE framework itself is a useful but limited instrument. While its four pillars pinpoint key levers of change within health systems, the framework leaves (by design) wide scope for local tailoring, and FIRE analyses are neither rigorously standardized nor exhaustive. The FIRE tool was not meant to replace other health system frameworks. Its pillars do not explicitly foreground many topics fundamental for health reform efforts in all settings, such as the health workforce, health information systems, and gendered differences in care needs and access, to name only a few. At the same time, the framework opens multiple spaces in which these and other topics can be considered, in line with country conditions and priorities. The national research teams have used FIRE flexibly, leveraging its strengths and balancing its limitations.

Gender is an especially salient lens through which population aging must be analyzed to gain a clear view of country realities. Women, on average, live longer than men, bear a disproportionate burden of informal care, have lower educational and labor force participation, and hence less financial security in old age. This situation translates to gendered differences in health care needs and patterns of use, which cannot be overlooked if countries want to reach inclusive policy solutions (Gatti et al. 2023; O'Keefe and Haldane 2023). In gender and other analytical areas, this collection of case studies therefore points to the need for further work.

Key Findings from the Case Studies

This section summarizes key results from the country and regional case studies, highlighting both the distinctive traits of individual studies and cross-cutting features.

Bangladesh: Reconfiguring Primary Health Care for an Aging Population

Bangladesh is home to one of the world's largest populations of older adults, and this population is growing as the country's life expectancy rises. By 2050, one in five Bangladeshis will be age 60 or above. This increase in lifespan is accompanied by a greater burden of noncommunicable diseases, which account for 70 percent of all deaths in the country. While the government has committed to protecting and providing the basic rights of older adults, health care needs among older Bangladeshis remain substantially unmet.

Bangladesh's PHC system is geared toward treating acute illnesses, rather than providing integrated, long-term, people-centered care for all, including older adults. This study aims to understand the current capacity of the PHC system to provide senior-oriented care in Bangladesh. It includes a desk review of global and Bangladeshi literature on aging populations; stakeholder consultations and interviews with key government officials, health professionals, and developmental organizations; and field visits to PHC facilities. Data were compiled and analyzed using the FIRE framework.

Despite its large burden of noncommunicable diseases, Bangladesh spends only US$0.82 per capita on NCD control, far below the US$1.50 recommended by the World Health Organization. Key support mechanisms are missing or inadequately supplied, such as a health insurance fund to cover common chronic conditions. Neither NCD control nor PHC services adequately consider older-adult needs. In regulation, several senior-specific policies have been adopted in principle but are not observed in practice. While there is motivation to evaluate the outcomes of service delivery for older adults, human resource shortfalls make this difficult.

The study presents recommendations for improving older-adult care in Bangladesh. The government can consider investing more in the health of older adults using an output-based budget. Cost-saving measures could be implemented in parallel, such as involving nonhealth ministries and enforcing clear guidelines on payment mechanisms. Leveraging digital health technology could improve access to care, while focusing on long-term care could improve older people's health outcomes. Additionally, training health professionals in an age-sensitive approach to care could improve the patient experience. Oversight could also play a vital role in improving the quality of care and accountability. To ensure a continuous supply of essential drugs, supply chain interruptions should be prevented. In health facilities, financial management policies could prevent waste, and an evaluation officer position could be created to monitor adherence to quality guidelines.

Colombia: Tackling Older-Adult Care Needs and Their Socioeconomic Determinants

An upper-middle-income country, Colombia is experiencing both demographic and epidemiological transitions, reflected in a rapidly growing older-adult population and rising morbidity and mortality from noncommunicable diseases.

Population aging in Colombia is characterized by the persistence of social inequities that result in health disparities and a precarious socioeconomic outlook for many older people. On paper, older Colombians are afforded special constitutional protections and have universal health coverage. In practice, many Colombians have difficulty accessing basic health services, housing, and nutritious food. Many older people's finances are strained by low employment rates, irregular employment, and low pension coverage.

This case study distills lessons learned during the design and implementation of policies for the health care of older persons in Colombia, highlighting key problems and identifying ways to address them. In particular, the establishment of a health model geared to the needs of older Colombians may require not only reforms in how health care is organized and delivered, but also a reconsideration of the social determinants of health outcomes.

Colombia's situation presents opportunities for improvement, particularly if leaders align policies and programs in older-adult care with the country's comprehensive 1993 health care reforms. The case study recommends strengthening institutional capacity to deliver Colombia's 2022–2031 National Public Policy on Aging and Old Age, notably by ensuring adequate and sustainable financing, leveraging the country's commitment to primary health care, and strengthening monitoring and evaluation capacity through the National Observatory on Aging and Old Age. The study highlights the importance of developing guidelines and care protocols to address geriatric syndromes and multiple morbidity through an interdisciplinary approach.

Mongolia: Expanding PHC-Based Older-Adult Services and Getting the Most from Screening Programs

Although Mongolia's population is relatively young, the number of adults ages 60 or older is rising steadily, and the prevalence of NCD risk factors among older Mongolians is high. Almost half of individuals 45–69 years of age are at high risk of developing a noncommunicable disease. Through a desk review and analysis of secondary data, the case study provides information on the country's PHC-centered integrated care systems for older adults using the FIRE framework. It also qualitatively assesses the implementation of an adult screening program and identifies further development needs.

In Mongolia, two types of facilities provide primary health care: family health centers and *soum* (administrative subdivision) health centers. The rural population is scattered across a vast land area. Primary health care is poorly implemented owing to a lack of human resources at PHC facilities, high workloads, and financial constraints. In general, PHC facilities lack services designed to maintain and improve older adults' basic functional abilities and intrinsic capacities. There is a need to ensure a continuum of care and to integrate screening with routine care.

The study recommends that health and nonhealth sectors strengthen their collaboration to build an environment in which older adults not only can meet their basic needs and enjoy an adequate standard of living, but also can learn, grow, make decisions, be mobile, build and maintain relationships, and actively contribute to society. Assessments are needed to identify the impacts of outdated versus modern attitudes toward age and aging, along with the prevalent types of ageism and discrimination against older adults, and to generate evidence that can inform policy actions. Finally, new financial and administrative mechanisms are needed to increase the participation of PHC facilities in delivering screening services to older people. This approach can reduce the workload of referral-level hospitals.

The United Arab Emirates: Harnessing a Crisis to Advance Integrated Older-Adult Care

Rising numbers of older adults pose challenges for routine health service delivery but also for the response to pandemics and other emergencies. In the United Arab Emirates, people ages 65 and older are projected to represent 16 percent of the population by 2050. This study details how the country's approach to health care for older people provided a foundation to tackle COVID-19, yielding innovations in service delivery that have proved useful beyond the crisis.

The case study highlights the Population-at-Risk Program in Abu Dhabi, the country's capital city. To limit COVID-19 infections among older adults and other vulnerable groups, the program deployed a hybrid service delivery model, combining virtual visits via a phone app–based telehealth platform with "at-your-doorstep care" through home visits, home delivery of medications, and home-based testing, both routine and COVID-19 related.

The Population-at-Risk Program turned the COVID-19 crisis into an opportunity to accelerate the use of digital health tools and engage public and private actors in protecting vulnerable people's health. On the one hand, the program faced challenges in the form of low patient digital literacy, people's discomfort with sharing personal health information in a virtual care setting, and a lack of provider resources. On the other hand, the program benefited from strong implementation of core public health measures such as physical distancing and testing and contact tracing, a well-structured health communications campaign, and rigorous program monitoring. In the wake of the crisis, health authorities are continuing to use and improve the Remote Healthcare Platform, opening it to more population groups. Lessons from the Abu Dhabi program may help other countries to enhance access, reduce costs, improve enrollment rates, and improve outcomes for older adults and high-risk patient groups.

Sub-Saharan Africa: Tailoring Older-Adult Care and Support Policies to Complex Demographic Profiles

The ratio of older Africans to the continent's total population is still relatively small and is rising more gradually than in other world regions. However, the absolute number of older Africans is enormous given the size of the continent's population, and this figure is projected to rise at a faster pace than in any other region between now and 2050. With the growing burden of noncommunicable diseases and rapid increase in older populations, older people's health and LTC needs will escalate across Africa in the coming decades. Family-based, informal support systems remain the backbone of long-term care for older Africans; however, these systems are increasingly strained and inadequate to meet the care needs of aging populations in the region as more and more traditional caregivers—namely women—are finding jobs outside the home. In most African countries, organized, formal, LTC services are hard to find, typically urban, and severely hindered by financing and workforce shortages. Some integrated care delivery models or programs do target older adults, but their sustainability is an issue.

Policy makers in Sub-Saharan Africa face the difficult challenge of managing multiple priorities with highly constrained resources. Although national policy is typically focused on alleviating poverty and expanding basic health insurance coverage for all, planning for and developing LTC services and their requisite policy frameworks need to begin sooner rather than later. As an overarching policy goal, a mixed, balanced LTC system that combines informal and formal services is desirable, with resource allocation tilted toward delivering services in older people's homes and in community settings while supporting the traditional practice of family caregiving.

In this context, it is advisable for policy makers to take an incremental and carefully sequenced approach to developing LTC systems. Countries can leverage existing PHC services to expand key components of long-term care progressively, for example, screening for noncommunicable diseases, nursing care, and help with medication management.

European Countries and Comparators: Evaluating and Measuring Data to Suggest Entry Points for Policy

Supporting older adults and other people with disabilities presents a growing challenge to care systems across the globe. Accurately assessing unmet needs is critical for effective response. Based on quantitative data on care needs and service provision from 31 countries, this study illustrates the power of evaluation and measurement in identifying policy levers to strengthen older-adult care.

The study evaluates the prevalence and extent of limitations in activities of daily living (ADLs) and instrumental activities of daily living (IADLs) and the availability of support for these limitations in 27 European countries and 4 comparator countries between 2011 and 2018.[6] The study also analyzes the demographic, social, and policy factors associated with ADL/IADL limitations and the provision of assistance to older adults. The results highlight significant variation among countries in the prevalence and extent of ADL/IADL limitations as well as differences in how the prevalence and extent of disabilities have changed over time. These variations can be attributed to country-level differences in socioeconomic conditions, health behaviors, chronic disease prevalence, and strength of public safety nets.

Although many of the study countries experienced an *increase* over time in the prevalence of ADL/IADL limitations, most countries showed a *decrease* in the percentage of older adults receiving assistance with ADL/IADL limitations—often because the population of older adults was growing. This finding suggests significant unmet need for ADL/IADL assistance among older adults. Although the factors associated with ADL/IADL limitations and the receipt of assistance differ by country, in most settings, age, partner status, income, and educational level are found to be significantly associated with ADL/IADL limitations. Specifically, unpartnered men are found to be less likely to receive help with ADL/IADL limitations. Countries may improve their health system outcomes by directing interventions toward vulnerable groups.

The Remainder of this Volume

The rest of this volume is structured as follows. Chapters 1 through 4 present country case studies from Bangladesh, Colombia, Mongolia, and the United Arab Emirates, respectively. Chapters 5 and 6 present the regional studies on Sub-Saharan Africa and European countries plus comparators, respectively. Chapter 7 steps back to draw high-level conclusions from the complete set of studies. It formulates policy recommendations under the four FIRE headings—financing, innovation, regulation, and evaluation—adopting an approach broadly similar to that used in shaping the conclusions of *Silver Opportunity*, Volume 1. A final chapter discusses how countries may advance the *Silver Opportunity* agenda in the years ahead, with support from the World Bank and other partners.

Notes

1. For information on the United Nations and World Health Organization initiative, visit https://www.who.int/initiatives/decade-of-healthy-ageing#:~:text=The%20 United%20Nations%20Decade%20of,communities%20in%20which%20they%20 live. Also refer to Shevelkova, Mattocks, and Lafortune (2023).
2. The estimated value of older adults' market and nonmarket contributions in a sample of European countries and the United States is equivalent to 7.3 percent of gross domestic product, while older adults make up 24 percent and 21 percent of the European and US populations, respectively (Bloom et al. 2020b).
3. The platform is available on the United Nations Decade of Healthy Ageing website, https://www.decadeofhealthyageing.org.
4. The original policy notes and papers can be accessed at https://documents .worldbank.org/en/publication/documents-reports/documentlist?colti=%22 silver%20opportunity%20case%20study%20series%22&srt=docdt&order=desc.
5. The analysis of the evolving Abu Dhabi Population-at-Risk Program in the United Arab Emirates study constitutes a partial exception to this pattern.
6. The global comparators are China, Israel, the United Kingdom, and the United States.

References

Bloom, David E., Alex Khoury, Eda Algur, and J. P. Sevilla. 2020a. "It's Time We Stopped Undervaluing Older Adults." *World Economic Forum* (online), December 7, 2020. https://www.weforum.org/agenda/2020/12/it-s-high-time-we-stopped -undervaluing-older-adults/.

Bloom, David E., Alex Khoury, Eda Algur, and J. P. Sevilla. 2020b. "Valuing Productive Non-Market Activities of Older Adults in Europe and the US." *De Economist* 168 (2): 153–81.

CSDH (Commission on Social Determinants of Health). 2008. *Closing the Gap in a Generation: Health Equity through Action on the Social Determinants of Health; Final Report of the Commission on Social Determinants of Health.* Geneva: World Health Organization.

Economist Impact. 2022. *Achieving Equitable Healthy Aging in Low- and Middle-Income Countries: The Aging Readiness & Competitiveness Report 4.0.* Washington, DC: AARP International.

Gatti, Roberta, Daniel Halim, Allen Hardiman, and Shuqiao Sun. 2023. "Gendered Responsibilities, Elderly Care, and Labor Supply: Evidence from Four Middle-Income

Countries." Background study for the World Bank Healthy Longevity Initiative, World Bank, Washington, DC.

Govindaraj, Ramesh, and Sundararajan Srinivasa Gopalan. 2023. "Control of Non-Communicable Diseases for Enhanced Human Capital: The Case for Whole-of-Society Action." Background study for the World Bank Healthy Longevity Initiative, World Bank, Washington, DC.

HLI (Healthy Longevity Initiative). Forthcoming. *Unlocking the Power of Healthy Longevity: Tackling Non-Communicable Diseases to Save Lives, Improve Wellbeing, Reduce Inequities, and Strengthen Human Capital.* Washington, DC: World Bank.

Horton, Richard. 2022. "Offline: How to Fix Pandemic Preparedness." *The Lancet* 399 (10339): 1927.

Hou, Xiaohui, Jigyasa Sharma, and Feng Zhao. 2023. *Silver Opportunity: Building Integrated Services for Older Adults around Primary Health Care.* Washington, DC: World Bank.

JICA (Japan International Cooperation Agency), Risa Nakayama, and Xiaohui Hou. 2023. "Community-Based Integrated Care in Japan." In *Silver Opportunity: Building Integrated Services for Older Adults around Primary Health Care*, edited by Xiaohui Hou, Jigyasa Sharma, and Feng Zhao, 159–78. Washington, DC: World Bank.

Kurowski, Christoph, David B. Evans, Ajay Tandon, Patrick Hoang-Vu Eozenou, Martin Schmidt, Alec Irwin, Jewelwayne Salcedo Cain, Eko Setyo Pambudi, and Iryna Postolovska. 2021. "From Double Shock to Double Recovery: Implications and Options for Health Financing in the Time of COVID-19." Health, Nutrition and Population Discussion Paper, World Bank Group, Washington, DC.

Kurowski, Christoph, David B. Evans, Ajay Tandon, Patrick Hoang-Vu Eozenou, Martin Schmidt, Alec Irwin, Jewelwayne Salcedo Cain, Eko Setyo Pambudi, and Iryna Postolovska. 2022. "From Double Shock to Double Recovery: Implications and Options for Health Financing in the Time of COVID-19. Second Technical Update: Old Scars, New Wounds." Health, Nutrition and Population Discussion Paper, World Bank Group, Washington, DC.

NAM (United States National Academy of Medicine). 2022. *Global Roadmap for Healthy Longevity*. Washington, DC: National Academies Press. https://doi.org/10.17226/26144.

NCD Countdown 2030 Collaborators. 2022. "NCD Countdown 2030: Efficient Pathways and Strategic Investments to Accelerate Progress towards the Sustainable Development Goal Target 3.4 in Low-income and Middle-income Countries." *The Lancet* 399: 1266–78.

O'Keefe, Philip, and Victoria Haldane. 2023. "Towards a Framework for Impact Pathways between NCDs, Human Capital and Healthy Longevity, Economic and Wellbeing Outcomes." Background study for the World Bank Healthy Longevity Initiative, World Bank, Washington, DC.

Scott, Andrew J. 2021. "The Longevity Economy." *The Lancet Healthy Longevity* 2 (12): e828–e835.

Shevelkova, Vlada, Colum Mattocks, and Louise Lafortune. 2023. "Efforts to Address the Sustainable Development Goals in Older Populations: A Scoping Review." *BMC Public Health* 23 (2023): 456. https://doi.org/10.1186/s12889-023-15308-4.

UN DESA (United Nations Department of Economic and Social Affairs). 2022. *World Population Prospects 2022: Summary of Results.* UN DESA/POP/2022/TR/NO. 3. New York: UNDESA, Population Division.

UN DESA (United Nations Department of Economic and Social Affairs). 2023. *World Social Report 2023: Leaving No One Behind in an Ageing World.* New York: UN DESA.

WHO (World Health Organization). 2015. *World Report on Ageing and Health.* Geneva: WHO.

WHO (World Health Organization). 2020. *Decade of Healthy Ageing Baseline Report*. Geneva: WHO.

WHO (World Health Organization). 2022. "Ageing and Health: Fact Sheet." WHO, Geneva. https://www.who.int/news-room/fact-sheets/detail/ageing-and-health#:~:text=By%202050%2C%20the%20world%27s%20population,2050%20to%20reach%20426%20million.

WHO (World Health Organization). Forthcoming. *World Report on the Social Determinants of Health Equity*. Geneva: WHO.

World Bank. 2022. *Change Cannot Wait: Building Resilient Health Systems in the Shadow of COVID-19*. Washington, DC: World Bank.

CHAPTER 1

Bangladesh: Reconfiguring Primary Health Care for an Aging Population

Khaleda Islam, Seemi Qaiser, Kathryn Andrews, Jigyasa Sharma, Xiaohui Hou, Bushra Binte Alam, and Atia Hossain

Key Messages

- By 2050, one in five Bangladeshis will be age 60 or older. Noncommunicable diseases (NCDs) now cause more than 70 percent of the country's deaths, and NCD burdens are rising fast.

- Bangladesh's primary health care (PHC) system remains geared toward treating acute illnesses, rather than providing integrated, people-centered prevention and care for chronic conditions, including in older adults.

- Bangladesh has introduced promising innovations, including dedicated NCD spaces in select PHC facilities. However, these models need more investment, rigorous evaluation, and scale-up if justified by results.

- Formal long-term care (LTC) for older people in Bangladesh is nascent. Other key support structures are also missing or undersupplied, including pensions and health insurance.

- Policies are recommended in the four FIRE domains: financing, innovation, regulation, and evaluation. For example, in evaluation and measurement, having a cadre of district-level "quality and coordination" officers who monitor adherence to quality guidelines could improve NCD care for older adults and other patients.

Background

Bangladesh is 1 of 20 low- and middle-income countries with the largest populations of older adults (defined as 60 years and older) in the world (Bangladesh Bureau of Statistics 2015). By 2025, Bangladesh, along with China, India, Indonesia, and Pakistan, will account for about half of the world's older-adult population, by which time 1 in 10 Bangladeshis will be age 60 or older. By 2050, 1 in 5 Bangladeshis will be 60 or older (Kabir et al. 2013). Given this rapid increase in the older population, aging is an increasingly important issue in Bangladesh, with potential long-term impacts on the country's development trajectory and its public service and health sectors.

Bangladesh's health sector, as of yet, is not fully prepared to support the needs of an aging population. As the older-adult population continues to grow, challenges are starting to emerge in the areas of health and social services. For one thing, as people age, the risk of developing noncommunicable diseases, which are costly to treat or manage for families in resource-poor countries, rises substantially (Sarker 2021). Such chronic conditions and multiple morbidity among older adults increase the demand for health care (Acharya et al. 2019). The diminishing physical and cognitive functions of the aging population, and hence their increasing dependency on others, will further increase the burden on families providing care (Kabir et al. 2013).

Compounding this situation, Bangladesh's health system will need to face the additional challenge of protecting older people from impending climate-related threats in the future. Climate change is poised to become the leading global risk factor for excess mortality (WHO and UN DESA 2022). Already prone to flooding, Bangladesh is expected to experience a significant increase in the frequency, duration, and intensity of heat stress, flooding, and landslides (World Bank 2022a). This increase in natural disaster activity will disproportionately affect the more vulnerable among the population, especially older adults (WHO and UN DESA 2022). Exposure to extreme weather events, especially those that require immediate evacuation, will likely take a toll on their physical and mental health (World Bank 2022a). The country largely is not prepared for this challenge.

New policies across the health and social sectors are therefore needed to support the older-adult population. Following the initiation of the United Nations Decade of Healthy Ageing (2021–30), the World Health Organization (WHO) led a global collaboration of governments, international agencies, civil society, and other stakeholders to focus on improving the lives of older people. One consensus that emerged from these collaborations is the recommendation that governments adopt the highest level of political commitment to ensure that their populations live long lives in good health—in short, a commitment to invest in their human capital. To address the basic need of health care for all, the World Health Organization recommends making primary health care the foundation for universal health coverage (WHO 2022a).

PHC facilities in Bangladesh are not oriented toward the health care needs of older adults. In 2013, Bangladesh developed a policy establishing the state's responsibility to secure the basic rights of older adults (Sarker 2021). However, in reality, this population must commonly contend with inadequate health care facilities, a lack of financial support, and negligence. The government should therefore start planning for an appropriate pension system and a health insurance scheme to cover the financial needs of this population. Most important, in alignment with WHO recommendations, the government needs to address the health care needs of the aging population through a PHC system, while planning for assisted-living facilities, adult day care centers, and other living supports (Bangladesh Bureau of Statistics 2015). Currently, Bangladesh's health care system focuses on curative care for acute illnesses and is not especially effective in addressing long-term care for chronic illness. Moreover, older adults need a wide range of health care services offered in a one-stop location—for example, in PHC facilities.

The Case Study Methodology

This study explores the capacity of Bangladesh's PHC services to provide integrated, long-term, people-centered care to older adults and presents recommendations for improving the infrastructure of care for aging adults by adopting a more integrated health care approach at the PHC level.

Qualitative data were collected through a literature review, field visits, key stakeholder consultations, and key informant interviews. A desk review of global and Bangladeshi research on aging populations was conducted, followed by stakeholder consultations and key informant interviews with government bureaucrats, health professionals who provide chronic care, and development partners. Additionally, field visits were conducted to understand and evaluate procedures and practices at the PHC facility level. Stakeholders who are directly related to chronic disease management and the Noncommunicable Disease Control Programme (NCDC) were also consulted. All data collected were compiled and analyzed along the thematic lines set out in the FIRE framework: (a) financing; (b) innovation (in digital health, competency of health workforce, supply of drugs, vaccines, technologies, assistive devices, service delivery); (c) regulation; and (d) evaluation.

Findings

Bangladesh's aging population is increasing. According to census data, from 2001 to 2022, the percentage of the population 60 years or older increased gradually and currently stands at 9.2 percent (figure 1.1) (Bangladesh Bureau of Statistics 2022).

In Bangladesh, life expectancy is rising, which means that the relative proportion of the population over 60 will continue to grow. Currently, life expectancy at birth is 73 years. As life expectancy rises, the number of years lived after age 60 will also rise (figure 1.2) (World Bank 2022b).

Population Age Structure

Bangladesh has a large proportion of youth 15–19 years old. According to 2022 census data, the largest proportion of the population is 15–19 years of age (10.3 percent) and the smallest is 95 years of age and older (less than 1 percent). Youths (age 15–24) made up 18.16 percent of the population in 2011, but 19.11 percent in 2022 (Bangladesh Bureau of Statistics 2022). Figure 1.3 shows the age-sex

FIGURE 1.1 Percentage of the Population Age 60 and Older in Bangladesh, 2001–22

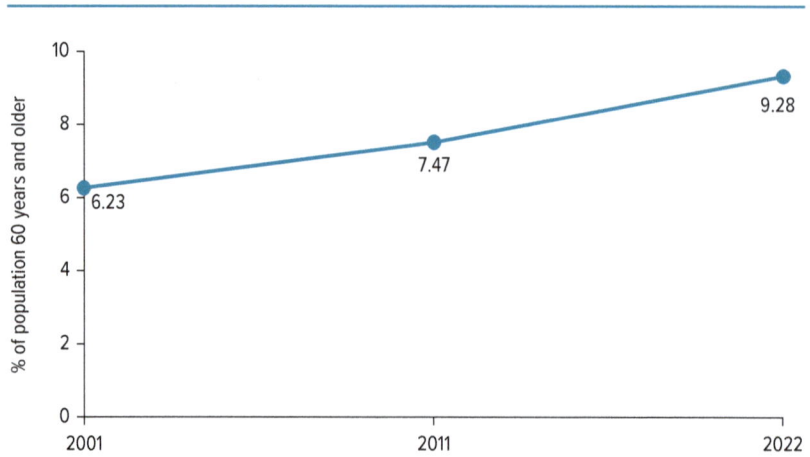

Source: Bangladesh Bureau of Statistics 2022.

FIGURE 1.2 Life Expectancy at Birth in Bangladesh, 1960–2020

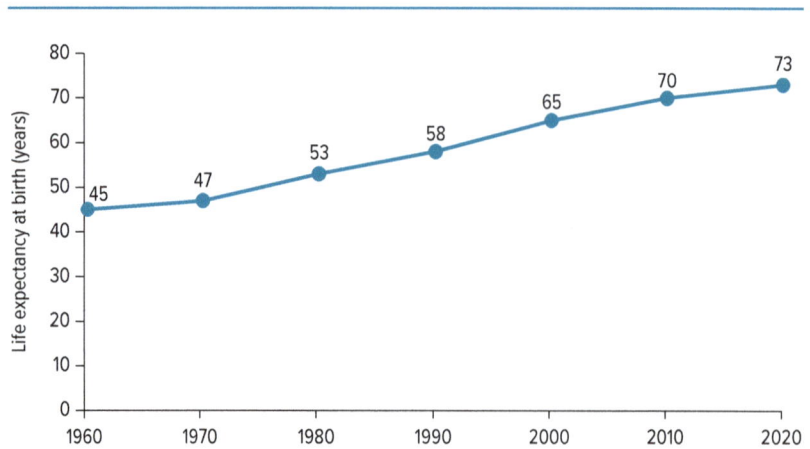

Source: World Bank 2022b.

pyramid in 2001, 2011, 2022, and 2051 (projected). The 2022 pyramid in panel c shows a shrinking base with a bulge in the lower middle. As shown in the progression from 2001 through 2051, the pyramid is becoming bell shaped due to the large number of young people (Bangladesh Bureau of Statistics 2022).

Bangladesh's low mortality and low, declining fertility are expected to cause a population boom by 2051 (Nabi 2012). Figure 1.4 presents the resulting age structure, by sex.

In 30 years, one in five Bangladeshis will be 60 or older. As of 2019, more than 13 million Bangladeshis—8 percent of the population—were 60 or older. As table 1.1 shows, the number of older persons will nearly triple by 2050—to about 36 million or 21.9 percent of the population (HelpAge International n.d.).

FIGURE 1.3 Age-Sex Pyramid in Bangladesh, 2001, 2011, 2022, and 2051 (Projected)

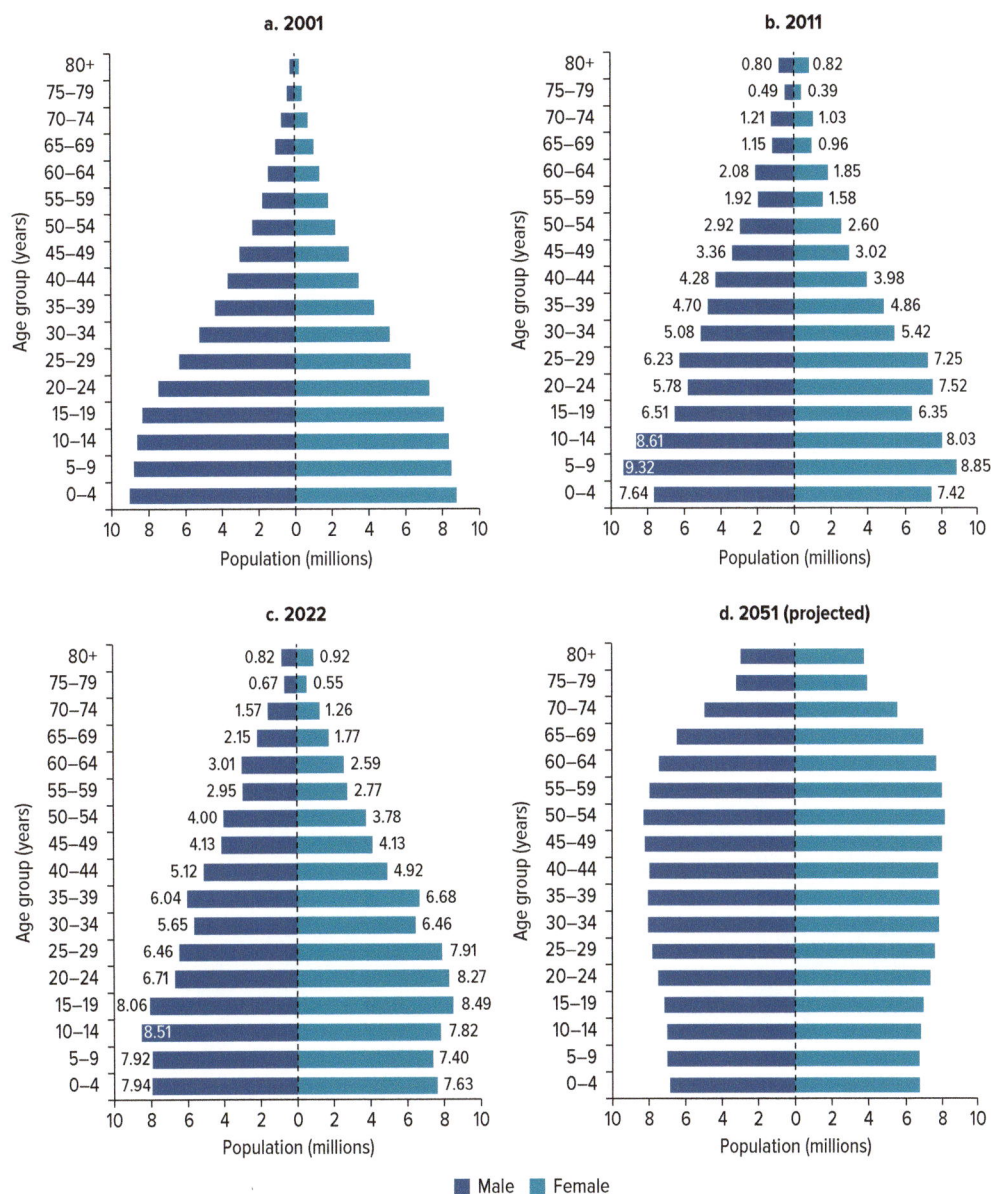

a. 2001

b. 2011

	Male	Female
80+	0.80	0.82
75–79	0.49	0.39
70–74	1.21	1.03
65–69	1.15	0.96
60–64	2.08	1.85
55–59	1.92	1.58
50–54	2.92	2.60
45–49	3.36	3.02
40–44	4.28	3.98
35–39	4.70	4.86
30–34	5.08	5.42
25–29	6.23	7.25
20–24	5.78	7.52
15–19	6.51	6.35
10–14	8.61	8.03
5–9	9.32	8.85
0–4	7.64	7.42

c. 2022

	Male	Female
80+	0.82	0.92
75–79	0.67	0.55
70–74	1.57	1.26
65–69	2.15	1.77
60–64	3.01	2.59
55–59	2.95	2.77
50–54	4.00	3.78
45–49	4.13	4.13
40–44	5.12	4.92
35–39	6.04	6.68
30–34	5.65	6.46
25–29	6.46	7.91
20–24	6.71	8.27
15–19	8.06	8.49
10–14	8.51	7.82
5–9	7.92	7.40
0–4	7.94	7.63

d. 2051 (projected)

■ Male   ■ Female

Sources: For panels b and c, Bangladesh Bureau of Statistics 2022. For panels a and d, Nabi 2012.

FIGURE 1.4 Population Age Structure, by Sex, in Bangladesh, 1990, 2019
(Reference Scenario), and 2100 (Reference Scenario)

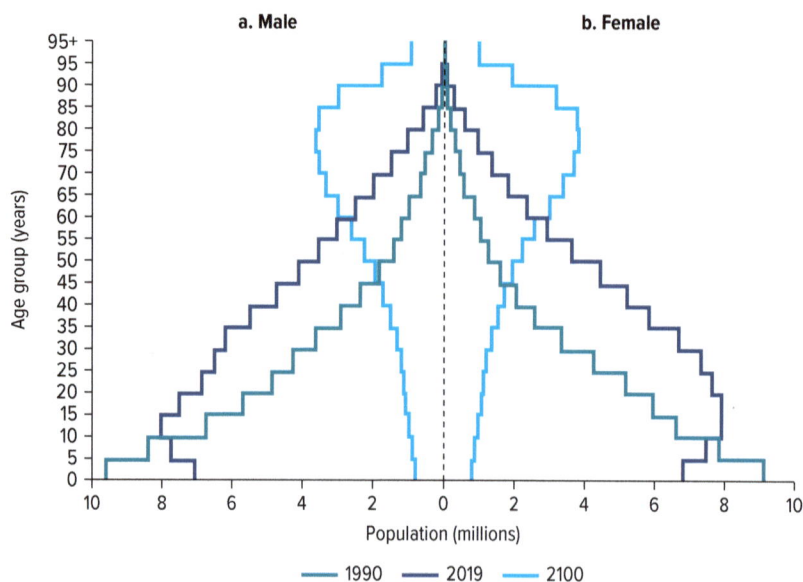

Source: GBD 2017 Disease and Injury Incidence and Prevalence Collaborators 2018.

TABLE 1.1 Aging Population in Bangladesh, 2019 and 2050 (Projected)

Indicator	2019	2050
Population age 60 and older (total)	13,109,000	36,871,000
Population age 60 and older (% of total population)	8.0	21.9
Older women age 60 and older (% of total population)	3.88	11.55
Life expectancy (male)	70.48	78.11
Life expectancy (female)	74.11	81.45
Old-age dependency ratio (age 65 and older / age 15–64)	7.7	23.5
Rural older people (% of total population)	3.46	—
Urban older people (% of total population)	1.4	—
Older persons living alone at age 60 and older (% of total population age 60 and older)	1.77	—

Source: HelpAge International n.d.
Note: – = not available.

Burden of Disease

Bangladesh is bearing the double burden of noncommunicable and communicable diseases. According to the World Health Organization, the proportional mortality (percent of total deaths, all ages, both sexes) from noncommunicable diseases is rising gradually and currently accounts for 70 percent of all deaths, an increase of 3 percent since 2018 (figures 1.5 and 1.6). The probability of

FIGURE 1.5 Proportional Mortality from Noncommunicable Diseases in Bangladesh, 2011–22

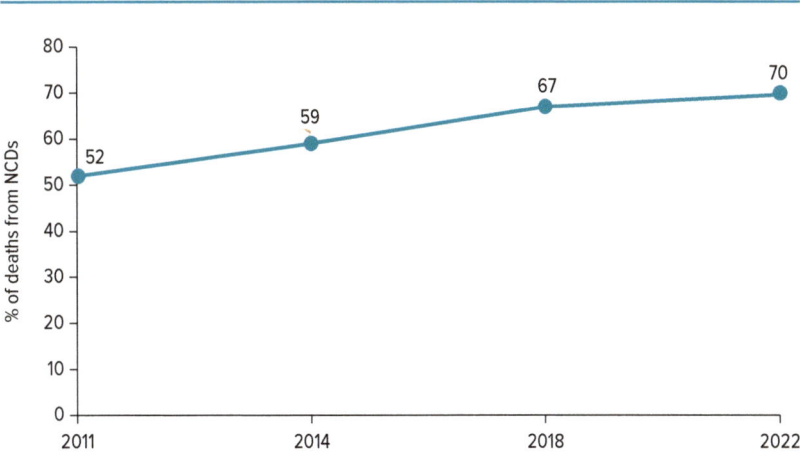

Sources: WHO 2011, 2014, 2018a, 2022b.
Note: NCD = noncommunicable disease.

FIGURE 1.6 Proportional Mortality from Various Causes in Bangladesh, 2018

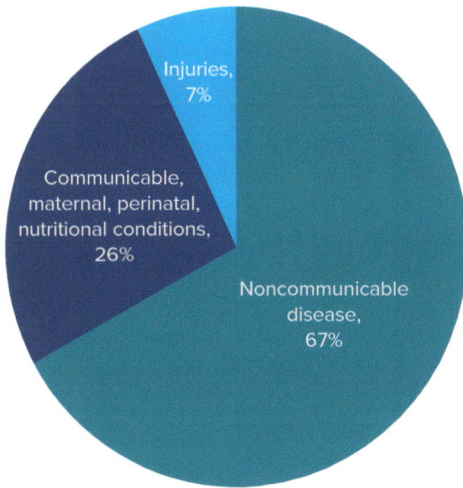

Source: WHO 2018b.

premature mortality from noncommunicable diseases is 19 percent (WHO 2011, 2014, 2018a, 2022b).

A study conducted in Bangladesh to explore the prevalence and pattern of multiple morbidity among persons 60 and older examined nine chronic health conditions (Khanam et al. 2011). The most common disorders were found to be arthritis (57.5 percent) and hypertension (38.7 percent) (table 1.2).

TABLE 1.2 Prevalence of Nine Chronic Health Conditions Used in Defining Multiple Morbidity in Bangladesh, by Sex, 2011

Chronic health condition	Total population		Men		Women		p-value
	Number	Percent	Number	Percent	Number	Percent	
Arthritis	260	57.5	113	55.4	147	59.3	0.231
Hypertension	175	38.7	74	36.3	101	40.7	0.192
Impaired vision	161	35.6	8	3.9	153	61.7	<0.0001
Signs of thyroid hypofunction	48	10.6	18	8.8	30	12.1	0.166
Obstructive pulmonary symptoms	31	6.9	27	13.2	4	1.6	<0.0001
Symptoms of heart failure	21	4.6	13	6.4	8	3.2	0.088
Hearing impairment	11	2.4	2	1.0	9	3.6	0.062
Obesity	11	2.4	3	1.5	8	3.2	0.186
Stroke	4	0.9	1	0.5	3	1.2	0.388

Source: Khanam et al. 2011.
Note: The sample size is 452: 204 men and 248 women. *p*-value is for the test of difference between men and women.

To determine the major causes of death among adults and seniors and their health care–seeking behavior, a study was conducted in the Matlab subdistrict of rural Bangladesh during 2003–04. Of the 2,397 deaths examined, 613 were of people 15–59 years old, and 1,784 were of adults 60 years of age and older. Communicable diseases caused 18 percent of all deaths, noncommunicable diseases caused 66 percent. As expected, the proportion of mortality attributable to noncommunicable diseases increased with age.

Despite a large NCD burden, Bangladesh does not have any NCD-specific policies in place. Given the importance of preventing and managing chronic disease, it is important for the government of Bangladesh not to fall into the trap of directing its policy-making processes to respond only to the loudest or most visible issues first; visibility does not necessarily equate to importance. Noncommunicable diseases, by their very nature, develop slowly and do not call attention to themselves—until they result in a crisis such as a stroke or in a debilitation that interferes with daily functioning. Like heart disease, noncommunicable diseases in general tend to be quiet killers, working invisibly in the background but eating away at the very foundation of a nation's human capital. The growing NCD burden in Bangladesh is a giant but silent scream.

Second, by their very nature, noncommunicable diseases are neither contagious nor infectious. People cannot catch them from others, which creates the false impression that they are a *private* individual matter. However, they are in fact a major, high-priority *public* health issue, even just from the point of view of their cost to the nation, including not only the cost of clinical treatment and management but also lost economic productivity and lost quality of life. As with climate change, it is important for the government to resist the temptation that has derailed many other governments—that is, the temptation to deprioritize an impending crisis that currently appears to be hidden from view.

Financing for Senior Care

The small budget allocated to health care is a significant problem in Bangladesh. In 2019–20, the health care budget was equal to 1.02 percent of gross national product (GDP). The public expenditure for health, population, and nutrition has remained unchanged, at 0.7 percent of GDP, for several years and needs to be increased. The government's eighth Five-Year Plan, July 2020–June 2025, recommends increasing the public expenditure on health, population, and nutrition and emphasizes the need to subsidize health insurance for seniors. The plan proposes increasing public health spending gradually to 2 percent of GDP by fiscal year 2041. It also suggests providing universal access to health insurance schemes at affordable prices as a means to achieve universal health care by 2030 (General Economics Division 2020).

Increasing national health spending to promote preventive care can help to mitigate the potential cost of expensive NCD curative treatment. According to the World Data Atlas (n.d.), in 2019, health care spending per capita was US$46 in Bangladesh. Moreover, Bangladesh's budget for NCD control was small, just 4.2 percent of the health sector program and equivalent to Tk 6.8 (Bangladesh taka) (US$0.082) per capita (World Bank 2019).

A study in Bangladesh in 2020 calculated that the annual cost of medication per patient with hypertension, diabetes, and high cholesterol was US$18, US$29, and US$37, respectively (Husain et al. 2022). The study recommended scaling up primary health care to prevent cardiovascular disease through task sharing—that is, shifting selected tasks from doctors to nurses and community health workers (Husain et al. 2022). This recommendation could be applied to other control programs to increase effectiveness, while containing costs.

The needs of the aging population are often overlooked in NCD financing and management. The current NCDC Operating Plan allocated an estimated budget of approximately US$140 million for the period January 2017 to June 2022. However, due to COVID-19, the implementation period of the fourth Health Population and Nutrition Sector Program, including the NCDC Operating Plan, was extended to June 2024. The NCDC Operating Plan focused on reducing morbidity and mortality from major noncommunicable diseases (Directorate General of Health Services 2017). The design of the NCDC Operating Plan emphasizes the prevention and management of major noncommunicable diseases (cardiovascular diseases, chronic respiratory diseases, diabetes, and cancer). Nevertheless, emphasis on aging care is insufficient.

Insufficient inputs include a shortage of drugs. Consultation with the *upazila* (subdistrict) health and family planning officer and team revealed that the budget allocation for medical and surgical requisites was approximately Tk 13.1 million (US$122,000) for the 2022/23 fiscal year. This allocation is based on in-patient capacity (number of beds) and use rates (bed occupancy rate). The assessment does not include outpatient care or patient turnover, which amounts to a significant gap in the data used to inform the budgeting and allocation process.

Innovation for Senior Care

The World Health Organization advocates a PHC approach and community involvement to ensure integrated people-centered health services for seniors. A review of care in rural PHC facilities showed that NCD care is available but lacks designated protocols for older adults (Kabir, Karim, and Billah 2023). In urban settings, primary health care is provided by the Ministry of Local Government, Rural Development, and Cooperatives and the Ministry of Health and Family Welfare, which focuses on care for mothers and children. Very limited palliative and rehabilitative care is present in Dhaka or in certain other cities. The private sector provides senior care at the secondary and tertiary levels, but it is comparatively expensive.

An inclusive, holistic approach is needed for senior health care. Too often the emphasis of health care policy and interventions focuses predominantly, or even exclusively, on the early years of life. But as demographics shift globally, health care policy and provision must also shift to prioritize good health at every age. The health and social needs of older adults should be assessed and integrated holistically into the design of people-centered health care. In addition, health workers need to be trained in information and communication technologies and older-adult care (WHO 2018a).

Integrated people-centered health services for seniors should be organized holistically around comprehensive health needs rather than the ad hoc, case-by-case treatment and maintenance of individual diseases. Integrated people-centered health services should also provide flexibility to accommodate social preferences because the more comfortable patients are, the more they open up to professional caregivers about their lives and lifestyle choices, which are often foundational to their health and determine the presence or absence of morbidities.

In 2019, a World Bank report found that noncommunicable diseases are responsible for 63 percent of disability-adjusted life years in Bangladesh (World Bank 2019). The report emphasized the importance of reorienting the health system toward integrated care for seniors with chronic conditions through a standardized and decentralized approach. The report further recommended sharing responsibilities between health care providers, community members or family members, and patients and achieving a fully integrated approach.

Seniors in rural areas encounter gaps in mental health services in PHC facilities, as rural PHC facilities do not have a mental health care package designated for seniors. Even in settings where patients receive support for managing noncommunicable and other chronic diseases, few services address the growing need for mental health support, including but not limited to counseling. The PHC protocol emphasizes drug dispensing and drug-compliance-related counseling for noncommunicable diseases but does not specifically mention mental health counseling (NCDC 2018b). No mental health care is offered in the *upazila* health complexes, a finding that aligns with a recent study (Islam et al. 2022).

Public primary health care in urban areas does not focus on NCD primary care. Urban primary health care is provided by the Ministry of Health and Family Welfare and the Ministry of Local Government, Rural Development, and Cooperatives through urban local government institutions (city corporations and municipalities). This care is supplemented by development partner–supported nongovernmental organizations and the private sector. But because of the limited resources of city corporations and the limited scope of the Ministry of Health and Family Welfare, the public sector has difficulty providing good-quality primary health care.

Although urban primary health care is mandated to provide a full package of essential services, the services are focused on maternal and child health and on sexual and reproductive health. Primary care for noncommunicable diseases is not prioritized in urban areas. Government facilities do not offer protocol-based NCD management and senior care. In a few urban areas, the Directorate General of Health Services, supported by development partners, has taken an innovative approach by providing all groups with a full range of essential services, including NCD care, during extended hours in PHC facilities. However, protocol-based NCD management—health care that is specific to older-adult needs—is absent. Very limited palliative and rehabilitative care is present in Dhaka and some other cities.

The private sector provides a full range of care for older adults, but it is expensive. Some organizations provide health insurance coverage for employees to supplement private health care expenses, but the coverage is very limited in scope and typically ends at retirement. Private health care is not available for free or reduced rates, even as part of corporate social responsibility.

Mechanisms for digital data collection are in place, but data are not disaggregated for seniors and nonseniors. NCD data are collected and managed as per the national protocol under the NCDC for hypertension and diabetes control, but different development partners support such activities with different types of software. For example, Resolve to Save Lives uses the open-source Simple App, whereas the International Centre for Diarrhoeal Disease Research, Bangladesh and Health and Education for All use proprietary software developed specifically for the organization. This situation leads to fragmentation of data collection and limits the potential for sharing and analyzing data across platforms.

The health workforce is not fully competent in delivering aging care. The NCDC provides training for health workers and orientation for managers to bolster NCD management at PHC facilities. The program applies a team-based approach to shifting and sharing tasks. However, health workers are not trained to deliver aging care, and there is no support system for caregivers and family members who provide elderly family members with long-term care.

The supply of drugs and diagnostics for NCD management at PHC facilities is unreliable. PHC protocols are followed, and insulin, inhalers, and antihypertensive, antidiabetic, antiplatelet, and lipid-lowering drugs have been added to the list of supplies, along with electronic blood pressure monitors and glucometers. However, equipment or assistive devices for long-term aging care are yet to be included in the supply list of PHC facilities. Ensuring supply chain management for senior-care-related drugs, diagnostics, and logistics remains a challenge. Usually, NCD drugs are supplied according to the NCDC Operating Plan, and shortages occur mostly in the last quarter of the year.

The shortage of health workers has a negative impact on the quality of service delivery. The NCDC leads NCD control and management, including activities to prevent risk factors. NCD corners[1] have been renovated in about 200 *upazila* health complexes to ensure protocol-based management of hypertension and diabetes with a team-based approach. Protocols have been developed for managing chronic respiratory diseases (asthma and chronic obstructive pulmonary diseases), screening for cervical cancer, providing palliative care, and managing or treating other diseases, including guidelines for disability. Community clinics provide refills of antihypertensive drugs to improve drug compliance by maintaining a more reliable, continuous supply.

No policy, strategy, or costed action plan related to senior health care has been developed to integrate senior long-term care into primary health care. At the national level, the government is planning to establish a geriatric hospital in Dhaka. One geriatric ward was established at Dhaka Medical College Hospital, but it was not operational at the time of the study.

At PHC facilities, patients receive services for common ailments that affect older adults—such as oral and eye concerns, osteoarthritis, chronic kidney conditions, chronic obstructive pulmonary disease, dementia, depression, and multiple morbidity. However, there is no arrangement for a one-stop shop that can meet several of the health needs of an older adult in one convenient physical location.

Regulations for Senior Care

Bangladesh does have some senior social protection policies, although senior health care–related policy, strategy, and action plans are largely nonexistent. The 69th World Health Assembly adopted a global strategy and action plan on aging and health and called on partners to (a) support and implement the strategy and plan, (b) improve the well-being of older persons and their caregivers with services, (c) support research and innovation, (d) exchange knowledge and innovative experiences, and (e) actively work on advocacy for healthy aging over the entire course of a person's life (WHO 2016).

In Bangladesh, policies and legislation are needed to ensure basic rights and improve the quality of life for the aging population. Although some health and social protection policies are specific to older adults, they are not sufficient to meet the basic needs of seniors, including housing, transportation, and recreation.

While efforts have been made to bring together multiple stakeholders across both the health and nonhealth sectors to collaborate on health care, they have not been as successful as expected. The Ministry of Health and Family Welfare is responsible for ensuring delivery of the essential services package through the rural and urban PHC system and referral care through secondary and tertiary facilities. Currently, the health care system is not adequately resourced or incentivized to implement integrated senior care. The NCDC has a multisectoral action plan for prevention and control of shared risk factors. However, the program has difficulty coordinating with stakeholders in nonhealth sectors (NCDC 2018a).

A National Multisectoral Coordination Committee was formed to implement the action plan, with the NCDC of the Directorate General of Health Services as the secretariat. The committee included about 30 ministries, institutes, and organizations. However, regular committee meetings did not occur as planned.

The Senior Care Program

Due to a shortage of human resources, the NCDC is unable to monitor and evaluate NCDC activities effectively. The program should consider evaluating the readiness of the service delivery system to implement Integrated Care for Older People (ICOPE) following the WHO guidelines. To support the implementation of ICOPE, the World Health Organization conducted a research project, the ICOPE implementation pilot program. The research and report will help countries, including Bangladesh, to evaluate the readiness of the service delivery system to implement ICOPE nationally (WHO 2018a).

The NCDC is an LTC program that implements hypertension and diabetes management in the NCD corner of *upazila* health complexes. Evaluation and ongoing monitoring of this program will ensure quality of care, coverage, and access. However, the shortage of health workers in the NCDC makes the evaluation component a significant challenge.

Recommendations

Financing

- *Provide adequate funding to implement integrated care for seniors.* This funding should cover the whole spectrum of preventive, promotive, curative, and rehabilitative activities at the community and facility levels.

Innovation

- *Improve recordkeeping for patient follow-up.* A dearth of individual and facility-based data, due to poor recordkeeping, was identified as a major constraint. The study urgently recommends digitizing the NCDC activities as quickly as possible.

- *Establish telemedicine care to expand access.* The Bangladesh health workforce should be equipped and trained with telehealth tools to extend the effectiveness of in-person visits and provide greater access and specialized care to older adults. The lack of good-quality health care service delivery was identified as a major concern. Digitization of NCDC activities will accelerate solutions to this problem.

Long-Term Care for Seniors in Primary Health Care

- *Provide senior-sensitive training for health workers.* Health workers need training specific to caring for older adults and the health issues that are common to the aging process, including management of multiple morbidity. Team-based care that shifts and shares tasks can shorten wait times and promote patient-centric care.

- *Redesign the service delivery system to center on senior care.* The essential services package should be updated to define senior care at facilities. PHC facilities should ensure a range of high-priority and targeted services, including waived registration fees, separate queues, and free diagnostic services for seniors.

- *Check patients for multiple morbidity and special health needs.* PHC facilities are an ideal, accessible place for older adults to be assessed for multiple morbidity, noncommunicable diseases, declining mental health, and geriatric syndromes. Geriatric syndromes are a group of complex, multifactorial health conditions prevalent in older people that generate a range of cognitive-behavioral impairments and functional limitations, strongly affecting quality of life. They include frailty, depression, urinary incontinence, polypharmacy, pressure ulcers, malnutrition, dizziness, reduced mobility that can lead to falls, syncope (fainting caused by a drop in blood pressure), and baseline cognitive impairment including delirium (sudden confusion, disorientation, and agitation). Intervention through regular checks at a local PHC facility can support individuals and families to manage geriatric syndromes and other conditions common to aging, such as hearing loss, vision loss and cataracts, back and neck pain, and osteoarthritis.

- *Offer health education and counseling for patients.* PHC facilities should use their patient waiting areas to offer information on topics such as healthy lifestyle tips, health risk prevention, and the importance of NCD screening. Counseling for older patients during visits should be introduced, especially for persons dealing with multiple morbidity and disability.

- *Provide emergency senior care at all levels: facility, community, and household.* Urban PHC facilities do not offer specialized senior care. This study recommends strengthening the urban PHC system to incorporate senior care by deploying more frontline health workers and improving coordination between the Ministry of Health and Family Welfare and the Ministry of Local Government, Rural Development, and Cooperatives.

- *Update the list of essential drugs and medical equipment.* The essential drugs list needs to be updated to support the delivery of essential services for older adults. The drugs should be affordable, generic, and tested for quality by the Directorate General of Drug Administration. Some assistive devices (eyewear, walking sticks, hearing aids, wheelchairs, prostheses, and so on) should be supplied free or at cost.

Regulation

- *Offer a training program for managers on financial regulation.* All managers from the NCDC and facilities should receive training in financial regulation, budget management, and other skills to facilitate the financial management of long-term care for older adults.

- *Pass regulations that improve the performance and accountability of health workers.* The recruitment, transfer, deputation, promotion, and other processes related to development of the health workforce to support older-adult health care should be free from political influence. Proper monitoring and supervision can ensure workforce accountability. Performance-based incentives should be introduced.

- *Prevent breaks in supply via supply chain management.* Effective supply chain management will ensure the timely supply of drugs, vaccines, technologies, and medical and surgical requisites. In addition, certified pharmacists should manage pharmacies and drug stores to advise on drug compatibility and adverse reactions, particularly for older adults.

- *Ensure quality across services via telemedicine regulations.* Proper regulation and quality checks of telemedicine services should be established to protect the aging population from substandard services.
- *Oversee the private sector in providing senior care.* The private sector should be subject to regular monitoring and supervision since its share of senior health care is substantial in Bangladesh.

Program Evaluation

- *Address gaps in program evaluation and perform quality assurance through monitoring and evaluation.* At the directorate level, the NCDC has only 10 program personnel, who therefore struggle with implementing the program and have little, if any, time for countrywide monitoring and supervision or evaluation.
- *Create a district-level NCD medical officer to monitor and evaluate the LTC program regularly.* Program activities that could be evaluated include the use of protocols and standard operating procedures, the availability of a trained health workforce, database maintenance, regular report generation, clinical audits, and follow-up of referral mechanisms.

Conclusion

A rapidly aging population and preexisting health system challenges mean that Bangladesh needs to plan strategically and reorganize its service delivery system to address the health care needs of older adults. While the government of Bangladesh has committed to providing many of the basic rights of older adults, the health care needs of seniors remain unmet. Primary and secondary data reveal deficits in the health system's capacity that will weaken the country's ability to address the health care challenges associated with its demographic shift. A lack of adequate funding and services points to the need for a health care system that caters to the specific needs of older adults, such as long-term care and consolidation of care. The PHC system, too, is geared toward treating acute illnesses rather than providing older Bangladeshis with integrated, long-term, people-centered care. On regulation, several senior-specific policies have been formally adopted but are not observed in practice. While there is motivation to evaluate the outcomes of service delivery for seniors, a shortage of human resources has made it difficult to carry out formal evaluations.

Bangladesh's demographic shift presents an important opportunity to rethink health care delivery to promote healthy aging. Levers such as strategic financing, innovations in service delivery, regulation, and evaluation and measurement can be deployed to identify and address the continually evolving needs of the senior population. Bangladesh has an opportunity to address aging-related population health and health system challenges, to drive health system reform, and to build a more inclusive and productive society.

Note

1. NCD corners are a dedicated platform for delivering NCD services at *upazila* health complexes. They were established in 2012 as part of the government's new initiative for addressing noncommunicable diseases.

References

Acharya, Sabnam, Saruna Ghimire, Eva M. Jeffers, and Naveen Shrestha. 2019. "Health Care Utilization and Health Care Expenditure of Nepali Older Adults." *Frontiers in Public Health* 7 (February 15, 2019): 24. https://doi.org/10.3389/fpubh.2019.00024.

Bangladesh Bureau of Statistics. 2015. *Elderly Population in Bangladesh: Current Features and Future Perspectives.* Dhaka: Bangladesh Bureau of Statistics, Statistics and Informatics Division, Ministry of Planning.

Bangladesh Bureau of Statistics. 2022. *Population & Housing Census 2022: Preliminary Report.* Dhaka: Bangladesh Bureau of Statistics, Statistics and Informatics Division, Ministry of Planning.

Directorate General of Health Services. 2017. *4th Health, Population and Nutrition Sector Programme: Operational Plan January 2017–June 2022.* Dhaka: Ministry of Health and Family Welfare, Health Services Division. http://hospitaldghs.gov.bd/wp-content /uploads/2020/01/HSM_OP_2017-22.pdf.

GBD 2017 Disease and Injury Incidence and Prevalence Collaborators. 2018. "Global, Regional, and National Incidence, Prevalence, and Years Lived with Disability for 354 Diseases and Injuries for 195 Countries and Territories, 1990–2017: A Systematic Analysis for the Global Burden of Disease Study 2017." *The Lancet* 392 (10159): 1789–858. https://doi.org/10.1016/S0140-6736(18)32279-7. Erratum in *Lancet* 393 (10190): e44.

General Economics Division. 2020. *Making Vision 2041 a Reality: Perspective Plan of Bangladesh 2021–2041.* Dhaka: Ministry of Planning, Planning Commission, General Economics Division. http://oldweb.lged.gov.bd/uploadeddocument/unitpublication/1 /1049/vision%202021-2041.pdf.

HelpAge International. n.d. "Ageing Population in Bangladesh." *HelpAge Asia.* https:// ageingasia.org/ageing-population-bangladesh.

Husain, Muhammad Jami, Mohammad Sabbur Haider, Renesa Tarannum, Shamim Jubayer, Mahfuzur Rahman Bhuiyan, Delinia Kostova, Andrew E. Moran, and Sohel Reza Choudhury. 2022. "Cost of Primary Care Approaches for Hypertension Management and Risk-Based Cardiovascular Disease Prevention in Bangladesh: A HEARTS Costing Tool Application." *BMJ Open* 12 (6): e061467. https://doi .org/10.1136/bmjopen-2022-061467.

Islam, Khaleda, Rumana Huque, K. M. Saif-Ur-Rahman, A. N. M. Ehtesham Kabir, and A. H. M. Enayet Hussain. 2022. "Implementation Status of Non-Communicable Disease Control Program at Primary Health Care Level in Bangladesh: Findings from a Qualitative Research." *Public Health in Practice* 3 (May): 100271. https://doi .org/10.1016/j.puhip.2022.100271.

Kabir, Russell, Hafiz T. A. Khan, Mohammad Kabir, and M. T. Rahman. 2013. "Population Ageing in Bangladesh and Its Implication on Health Care." *European Journal of Scientific Research* 9 (33): 34–47. https://doi.org/10.19044/esj.2013.v9n33p%25p.

Kabir, Ashraful, Md Nazmul Karim, and Baki Billah. 2023. "The Capacity of Primary Healthcare Facilities in Bangladesh to Prevent and Control Non-Communicable Diseases." *BMC Primary Care* 24: 60. https://doi.org/10.1186% 2Fs12875-023-02016-6.

Khanam, Masuma A., Peter K. Streatfield, Zarina N. Kabir, Chengxuan Qiu, Christel Cornelius, and Åke Wahlin. 2011. "Prevalence and Patterns of Multimorbidity among

Elderly People in Rural Bangladesh: A Cross-Sectional Study." *Journal of Health, Population, and Nutrition* 29 (4): 406–14. https://doi.org/10.3329/jhpn.v29i4.8458.

Nabi, A. H. M. Nurun. 2012. "Demographic Trends in Bangladesh." Paper presented at a Department of Population Sciences University of Dhaka seminar. http://www.iedcr .org/pdf/files/NPHC%20WEB/UPLOAD-4/Dr.Nurun%20Nabi.pdf.

NCDC (Non-Communicable Disease Control Programme). 2018b. *Multisectoral Action Plan for Prevention and Control of Noncommunicable Diseases 2018–2025.* Dhaka: Ministry of Health and Family Welfare, Directorate General of Health Services.

NCDC (Non-Communicable Disease Control Programme). 2018a. *National Protocol for Management of Diabetes and Hypertension: Integrated Management of High Blood Pressure, Diabetes, and High Cholesterol Using a Total Cardiovascular Risk Approach.* Dhaka: Ministry of Health and Family Welfare, Directorate General of Health Services. https://ncdc.gov.bd/storage/app/public/uploads/program/546090322054340.pdf.

Sarker, Abdur Razzaque. 2021. "Health-Related Quality of Life among Older Citizens in Bangladesh." *SSM—Mental Health* 1 (December): 100031.

WHO (World Health Organization). 2011. *Noncommunicable Diseases Country Profiles 2011.* Geneva: WHO. https://apps.who.int/iris/handle/10665/44704.

WHO (World Health Organization). 2014. *Noncommunicable Diseases Country Profiles 2014.* Geneva: WHO. https://apps.who.int/iris/handle/10665/128038.

WHO (World Health Organization). 2016. *Global Strategy and Action Plan on Ageing and Health (2016–2020): A Framework for Coordinated Global Action by the World Health Organization, Member States, and Partners across the Sustainable Development Goals.* Geneva: WHO. https://cdn.who.int/media/docs/default-source/mca-documents /ageing/gsap-summary-en.pdf?sfvrsn=b1ef0fae_5&download=true.

WHO (World Health Organization). 2018a. *Integrated Care for Older People (ICOPE): Realigning Primary Health Care to Respond to Population Ageing.* Geneva: WHO. https://www.who.int/publications-detail-redirect/WHO-HIS-SDS-2018.44.

WHO (World Health Organization). 2018b. *Noncommunicable Diseases Country Profiles 2018.* Geneva: WHO. https://apps.who.int/iris/handle/10665/274512.

WHO (World Health Organization). 2022a. *Building Leadership and Capacity for the UN Decade of Healthy Ageing (2021–2030).* Geneva: WHO. https://www.who.int/activities /building-leadership-and-capacity-for-the-un-decade-of-healthy-ageing-(2021-2030).

WHO (World Health Organization). 2022b. *Noncommunicable Diseases: Progress Monitor 2022.* Geneva: WHO. https://apps.who.int/iris/handle/10665/353048.

WHO (World Health Organization) and UN DESA (United Nations Department of Economic and Social Affairs). 2022. *The UN Decade of Healthy Ageing 2021–2030 in a Climate-Changing World.* Geneva: WHO; New York: UN DESA. https://cdn.who .int/media/docs/default-source/decade-of-healthy-ageing/decade-connection-series -climatechange.pdf?sfvrsn=e926d220_4&download=true.

World Bank. 2019. *The Continuum of Care for NCDs in Bangladesh: The Time to Act Is NOW!* Washington, DC: World Bank Group. https://documents.worldbank.org/en /publication/documents-reports/documentdetail/846731579019569888/The -Continuum-of-Care-for-NCDs-in-Bangladesh-The-Time-to-Act-is-NOW.

World Bank. 2022a. *Bangladesh: Country Climate and Development Report.* Washington, DC: World Bank Group. https://openknowledge.worldbank.org/bitstream/handle /10986/38181/CCDR-Bangladesh-MainReport.pdf.

World Bank. 2022b. "Life Expectancy at Birth, Total (Years)—Bangladesh." World Bank DataBank (database). World Bank, Washington, DC. https://data.worldbank.org /indicator/SP.DYN.LE00.IN?locations=BD.

World Data Atlas. n.d. "Bangladesh—Current Expenditure on Health Per Capita, 1960–2021." World Data Atlas (data hub). Knoema, Washington, DC. https:// knoema.com//atlas/Bangladesh/topics/Health/Health-Expenditure/Health -expenditure-per-capita.

CHAPTER 2

Colombia: Tackling Older-Adult Care Needs and Their Socioeconomic Determinants

Lenis Urquijo, Jose Valderrama, Juan Arango, and
Juan Pablo Toro

Key Messages

- An upper-middle-income country, Colombia is experiencing rapid growth in its older-adult population, along with rising morbidity and mortality from noncommunicable diseases (NCDs).

- Population aging in Colombia is characterized by socioeconomic inequalities that fuel health disparities. Older Colombians with lower incomes face disproportionate disability and mortality, compared to their wealthier compatriots. Improving health for all older Colombians is likely to require both health care reforms and stronger action on the social determinants of health.

- Bogotá's new District Care System for older people opens promising directions. Introduced in 2020, the District Care model leverages informal care resources present in communities and seeks to advance gender equity in older-adult care.

- Monitoring and evaluation are critical to achieving Colombia's healthy-longevity goals. The country can improve the impact of its policies and programs by continuing to strengthen its evaluation capacities through the National Observatory on Aging and Old Age.

Background

Colombia is an upper-middle-income country experiencing both demographic and epidemiological transitions that are driving a rise in aging as well as morbidity and mortality from chronic noncommunicable diseases. In 2021, an estimated 7.1 million Colombians—13.9 percent of the population—were elderly (60 years and older). By 2030, the number of elderly will increase to 9.7 million and constitute 17.5 percent of the population (Decree 681 of 2022). From 2020 to 2025, life expectancy for Colombians is expected to be 76.01 years, compared to an average of 74 years for all upper-middle-income countries—a significant increase from the 66.76 years recorded over the 1985–90 period (Ministry of Health and Social Protection 2021a).

The latest study of the burden of disease, conducted in 2010 and published in 2014, found that four noncommunicable diseases—cardiovascular disease, cancer, chronic respiratory disease, and diabetes—account for 82 percent of NCD deaths in Colombia (Peñaloza et al. 2014). According to the National Policy on Aging and Old Age, the prevalence of chronic noncommunicable diseases in older adults is 40 percent (Peñaloza et al. 2014).

In Colombia, the aging process is influenced by a persistence of social inequities that result in health inequalities and hence a precarious socioeconomic outlook for many older people (Arrubla 2014). Despite the fact that Colombia's government affords older persons special constitutional protections (Ministry of Health and Social Protection 2015) and provides universal health coverage, in practice, Colombia's elderly have difficulty accessing basic health services, housing, and high-quality food. Additionally, their finances are strained by irregular or low employment rates and low pension coverage (Ministry of Health and Social Protection 2015).

Colombia has an opportunity to improve this situation by implementing public policies, programs, and interventions for the care of older adults that are modeled on comprehensive health care reforms introduced in 1993 in Bogotá. Those 1993 reforms in health care and social services for older adults involved different levels of government, the private sector, communities, and households and were designed to meet the complex demands of elder care. These measures include a comprehensive package of health care reforms that introduced mandatory national social health insurance, health benefits packages, the promotion of competition, and managed care. However, there is room for improvement in the coverage of social benefits and access to pensions.

The Landscape of Aging and Old Age in Colombia

The Colombian population has experienced rapid aging in the last two decades, as evidenced by changes in the population pyramid and population indexes (table 2.1). The demographic transition has accelerated: the population ages 60 and older grew from 2.14 million in 1985 to 5.75 million in 2018, an annual growth of 3.5 percent, which is substantially higher than the 1.7 percent growth rate of the total population (DANE 2022).

As evident in figure 2.1, the broad-based pyramid of 1985 (solid blue) was transformed into a narrower-based structure by 2018 (DANE 2022).

TABLE 2.1 Demographic Indexes of Colombia, 2018–23

Demographic index	2018	2019	2023
Childhood index	24	23	23
Youth index	26	25	24
Old-age index	13	14	15
Aging index	54	60	65
Demographic dependency index	48.88	48.76	49.05
Child dependency index	35.77	34.54	33.8
Higher dependency ratio	13.10	14.22	15.26
Friz index	121.86	114.97	110.04

Source: Ministry of Health and Social Protection 2021b.
Note: The childhood index is the ratio of children under 15 to total population. The youth index is the ratio of people ages 15–29 to total population. The old-age index is the ratio of population older than 65 to total population. The aging index is the ratio of older adults to number of children and young people. The demographic dependency index is the ratio of population under 15 and over 65 to population ages 15–64. The child dependency index is the ratio of population under 15 years to population ages 15–64. The higher dependency ratio is the ratio of population over 65 to population ages 15–64. The Friz index is the ratio of population under 20 years to population ages 30–49. When the Friz index exceeds 160, the population is considered to be young; when the index is less than 60, the population is considered to be aging.

FIGURE 2.1 Census Data for Colombia, 1985 and 2018

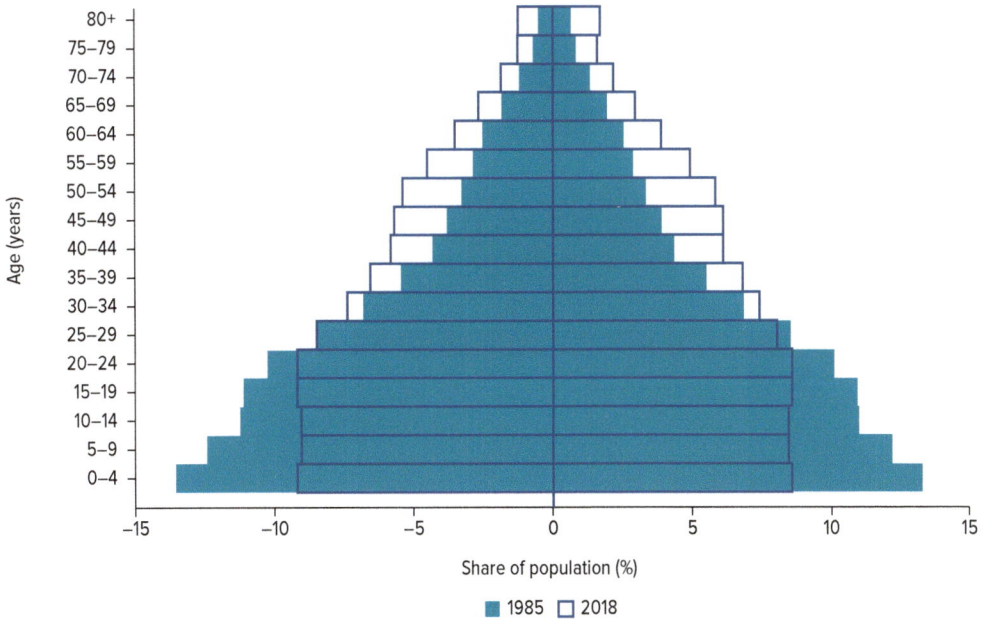

Source: Ministry of Health and Social Protection 2018.

This population aging is driven by a combination of a large decrease in fertility rates and a decline in mortality rates resulting in an increase in life expectancy rates.

Geographically, the elderly population is concentrated in the center of the country and in municipalities (map 2.1). In 2021, 77.3 percent of older adults lived in municipal capitals, with the remaining 22.7 percent living in rural areas (Decree 681 of 2022). According to the 2018 census, large cities and departments of the Andean zone have most of the elderly population. The departments with the highest proportion of older adults among their population are Quindío (19.7 percent), Caldas (19.3 percent), Risaralda (18.4 percent), Bogotá (15.5 percent), Antioquia (14.2 percent), and Valle del Cauca (10.5 percent). The departments with the lowest proportion are Vichada (6.1 percent), Guainía (6.1 percent), and Vaupés (6.2 percent).

MAP 2.1 Proportion of the Elderly Population in Colombia by Territorial Entity, 2020

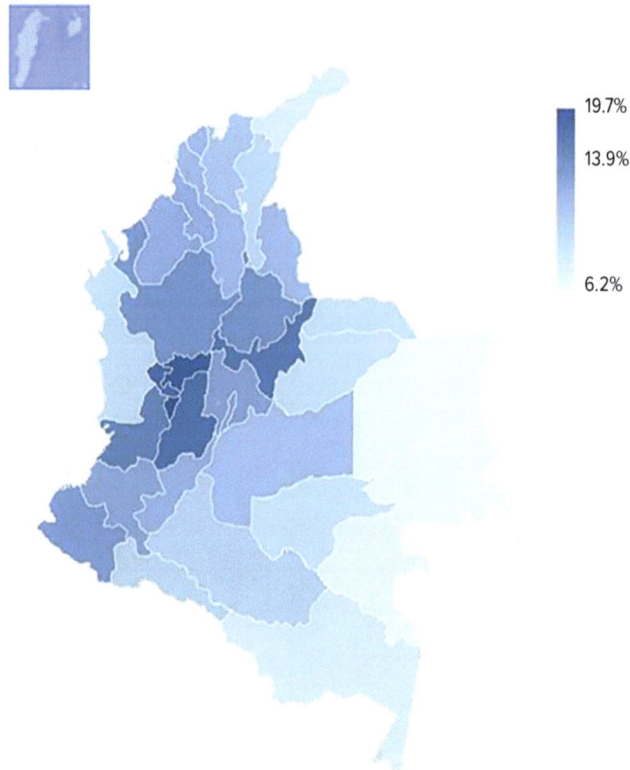

19.7%

13.9%

6.2%

Source: DANE 2022.

Women (3.9 million) constitute 55.1 percent of the population ages 60 and older, and men (3.2 million) constitute 44.9 percent (figure 2.2). The 2015 Health, Wellness, and Aging survey (SABE)[1] determined that 83.9 percent of persons who care for older adults are women ranging from 18 to 88 years old, with an average age of 49; 16.7 percent of these female caregivers are 60 or older (Ministry of Health and Social Protection 2015).

Activities of daily living (ADLs) deteriorate with age. The 2015 SABE found that 79 percent of the elderly population are independent in their basic ADLs and that dependency is greater among older women and among older people at lower socioeconomic levels (Ministry of Health and Social Protection 2015). The survey also found that 2.2 percent of people ages 60 or older have severe or total dependence, and 19.1 percent have mild or moderate dependence.[2]

The study additionally found that a quarter of the elderly have no income, while 55 percent of those with income indicated that it is below a minimum wage (figure 2.3). A high proportion of older adults in the Amazonia and Orinoquía regions (53.4 percent) and the Caribbean region (47.3 percent) are in stratum 1[3] (the lowest level of economic capacity). About 40 percent of older people in the Eastern, Central, Pacific, and Bogotá regions are in stratum 2. The highest proportion of older adults in strata 3 to 4 (50.8 percent) are in Bogotá.

In rural areas, 57.6 percent of older adults are in stratum 1. Such socioeconomic disadvantage has pronounced implications for health and quality of life. For example, persons living in poorer areas die up to six years earlier than those

FIGURE 2.2 Percentage of People Age 60 and Older in Colombia, by Age Group and Sex, 2015

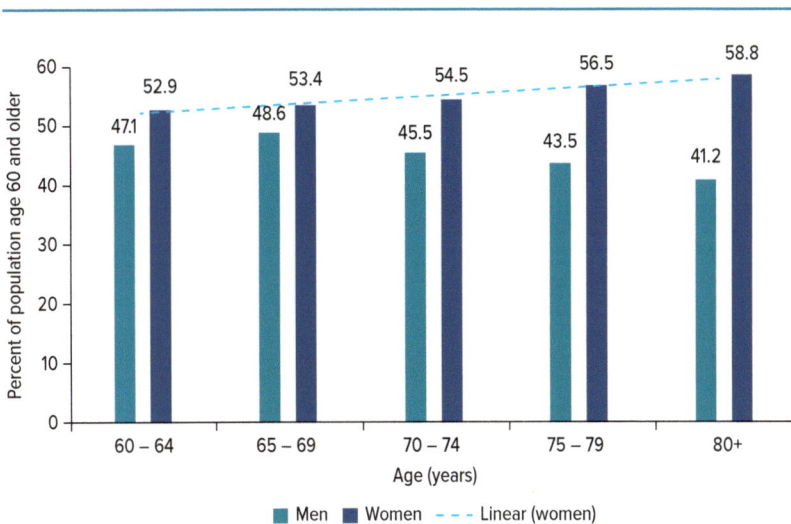

Source: Ministry of Health and Social Protection 2015.

FIGURE 2.3 Percentage of Colombians Age 60 and Older, by Socioeconomic Status, 2015

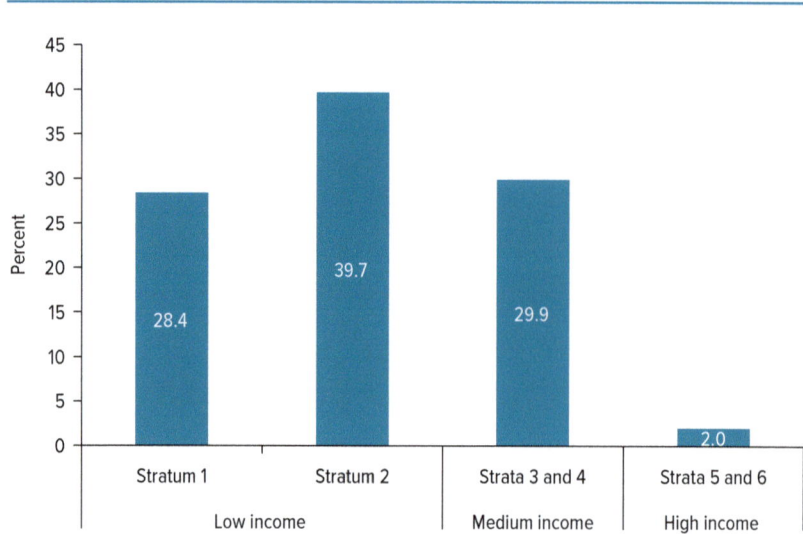

Source: Ministry of Health and Social Protection 2015.
Note: Strata are rankings of residential properties by income for the purpose of determining differential charges and subsidies for public utility services.

living in areas with greater economic resources (Ministry of Health and Social Protection 2015).

The aging population faces significant barriers to accessing health services. Chronic conditions have the highest prevalence of morbidity among older adults. Access to services such as breast and prostate cancer treatment is very low. According to the 2015 SABE, the chronic conditions in table 2.2 are the most frequent pathologies among Colombia's older adults (Ministry of Health and Social Protection 2015).

Regarding the use of health services among older adults, the survey revealed the following:

- 74.4 percent reported using ambulatory health services in the 30 days before the survey.

- 94.9 percent reported using ambulatory health services to reach general medicine or specialized medicine care.

- 58.7 percent of women had not had a mammogram in the last two years.

- In the preceding two years, 54.3 percent of men had not undergone a digital rectal exam for early detection of prostate cancer, and 53.7 percent had not had a prostate antigen test.

- 44.3 percent considered that the care they received was not very good or good.

Older adults with disabilities identify the unavailability of health professionals as the largest obstacle to accessing health services, followed by the unavailability of procedures and the delivery of medicines.

TABLE 2.2 Most Frequent Pathologies among Colombia's Older Adults

Chronic condition	Prevalence (%)	Notes
Visual impairment	88.9	67.0% reported wearing glasses or contact lenses
Hypertension	60.7	
Depression	41.0	
Hearing impairment	27.2	2.6% reported using devices such as hearing aids
Diabetes mellitus	18.5	
Ischemic heart disease	14.5	
Osteoporosis	11.8	
Chronic lung disease	11.4	
Cancer	5.3	Most frequently reported by men: prostate, skin, and stomach cancer. Most frequently reported by women: cervix, breast, and skin cancer.
Cerebrovascular disease	4.7	

Source: Ministry of Health and Social Protection 2015.

The 2015 SABE also records that psychological, physical, financial, and sexual abuse of older adults is not uncommon: 12.3 percent—roughly one in eight—reported being the victim of abuse. The national rate of violence against older adults was 36.4 per 100,000 residents in 2019 (Ministry of Health and Social Protection 2015).

On June 28, 2022, when the Colombian Truth Commission released its final report on the country's long-standing armed conflict between the government, far-right paramilitary groups, far-left guerrilla groups, and crime syndicates, it was revealed that, between 1985 and 2018, 450,666 people, including more than 177,000 civilians and 45,000 children, were killed in the conflict; 121,768 people disappeared, including 50,770 who were kidnapped; 16,238 children were recruited to fight; and more than 7.75 million Colombians were forcibly displaced from their homes, including 2.3 million children (Colombian Truth Commission 2022; Fleck 2022). Many members of this population likely require psychological counseling.

The Registry of Health Care Workers in Health identifies 1,073 registered professionals and 69 specialists in geriatrics (35 men and 34 women). According to the Information System of Education for Work and Human Development, Colombia has 1,269 training programs to obtain a technical labor certification in care, assistance, and comprehensive care for the elderly as a geriatric home assistant or specialist in geriatrics and gerontology. Recently, the training centers of the National Learning Service launched an in-person course on the need of older people for comprehensive care (Decree 681 of 2022).

Many older adults serve as caregivers for children ages 5 or younger in their home settings. Thus, when mothers between the ages of 13 and 49 work outside the home, 42.7 percent of their children are cared for by their grandparents (Ministry of Health and Social Protection and Profamilia 2015).

The SABE indicates that 63 percent of older people live in their own home, but 11 percent live in overcrowded conditions. Fifty-two percent use public transportation as their main means of transportation, a quarter require help in transportation, and around two-thirds require dental prostheses.

Since the beginning of the COVID-19 pandemic, a total of 1,002,587 elderly Colombians have been infected with COVID-19, corresponding to 15.8 percent of total cases (6,349,971), as of January 15, 2023. The mortality rate is higher in this population than in other age groups: of 142,259 COVID-19 deaths, 73.7 percent (104,912) were among the elderly. Being older, having at least one comorbidity, and being overweight or obese are the main predictors of severe COVID-19 cases in Colombia.

Health system coverage is almost universal for older adults.[4] However, coverage does not guarantee effective access to health services. In 2022, coverage of older adults was at the same level as coverage of the general population, at 96 percent. According to the Unified Database of Affiliation to the Health System, 47.8 percent of Colombians over 60 are under the subsidized regime, 46.3 percent are in the contributory regime, and 5.9 percent are in special regimes.

Colombia has various mechanisms for monitoring and following up on older adults, but they require strengthening and continuity. In August 2022, the Ministry of Health and Social Protection introduced the National Observatory on Aging and Old Age (ONEV) to support implementation of the Public Policy on Human Aging and Old Age within the framework of Colombia's accession to the Inter-American Convention on the Protection of the Human Rights of Older Persons. According to the Ministry of Health and Social Protection (2022),

> [The] ONEV contributes to the expansion of the body of knowledge on the determinants of aging and the living conditions of people 60 years and over in Colombia, as well as on the successful experiences of intervention in the promotion, prevention, and comprehensive care of this population group, managing, analyzing, and having the relevant information to improve decision-making that contributes to improving their well-being.

The ONEV's goal is to become, by 2023, the main compiler and reference source of the information on aging and old age in Colombia. For monitoring, follow-up, and evaluation of the National Public Policy on Aging and Old Age 2022–2031, the ONEV proposes the following thematic lines:

- Demographic aging and population structure
- Determinants of aging and old age
- Violence against people ages 60 and older
- Living conditions of people ages 60 and older
- Follow-up and monitoring of public policy
- A differential approach.

Regulation

In Colombia, elderly people have broad constitutional and legal protections. Nonetheless, this protection has not been fully developed, and challenges remain in implementation and coverage. Article 46 of the Constitution establishes the responsibilities of the government, the society, and the family to protect and assist this population, including the obligation to guarantee comprehensive social security services and food subsidies in case of indigence (Corte Constitucional 1991).

Colombia has a general social security system in health, which includes rules for the health system, insurance, and the pension system. The health system is based on an insurance system whose objective is to guarantee access to health services and the economic protection of the population. It has a high level of specialization among its various actors, which include central and territorial entities and public and private companies. The beneficiaries are affiliated with the insurance companies (through the Entidades Promotoras de Salud) that represent them and manage their health risks, coordinating the necessary services, as determined by the Benefits Plan. The Benefits Plan refers to the eligible range of services, procedures, drugs, and technologies to prevent, alleviate, and treat diseases. Other regulations address the protection of lower-income older adults through additional funding sources for the provision, operation, and development of prevention and promotion programs at elderly welfare centers and life centers for the elderly and the preferential treatment of such adults in education, employment, recreation, and living conditions (Law 687 of 2001 and Resolutions 024 of 2017 and 055 of 2018; Ministry of Health and Social Protection 2017, 2018).

In September 2020, Colombia acceded to the Inter-American Convention on the Protection of the Human Rights of Older Persons of June 2015. This instrument states that older adults have the same human rights, freedoms, and dignity as everyone else and that they must be allowed to continue to enjoy—to the extent possible—full, independent, and autonomous lives in which they experience health, safety, integration, and active participation in the economic, social, cultural, and political spheres. In May 2022, in accordance with the convention, the National Policy on Aging and Old Age 2022–2031 was issued (Decree 681 of 2022). This policy requires formulation of the National Intersectoral Action Plan, creation of the National Observatory on Aging and Old Age, operationalization of the National Council for the Elderly, and articulation of the Ten-Year Public Health Plan 2022–2031.

Design and Implementation of Public Policies on Aging and Old Age

Colombia has enacted three policies on aging and old age over the years, but there is ample room for improvement in implementing their objectives. The most recent policy was adopted through Decree 681 of 2022, which establishes an intersectoral framework for managing activities of interest to the elderly. The formulation of this policy took into account the progress and challenges of previous policy proposals and was the result of broad social participation, including the participation of the National Council of Older Persons, created by Decree 163 of 2021.

The government has defined the current pension age in law as 57 years for women and 62 for men. To access the pension, a person must have contributed throughout his or her working life (approximately 26 years).[5] But given the high levels of informal work in Colombia—as of November 2023–January 2024, 55.7 percent of employed people worked in the informal sector (DANE 2024)—the pension coverage of the elderly is very low, approximately 25 percent, compared to approximately 80 percent in countries such as Chile and the United States (Parra et al. 2020). In response, over the last two decades the country has developed complementary financial mechanisms to protect the vulnerable elderly population, including the following:

- *Colombia Mayor* (Elderly Colombia), which is a subsidy program for older people living in extreme poverty
- Periodic Economic Benefits Program, which was created in 2005 to provide an alternative security mechanism for the elderly population who reach the required retirement age but have not contributed enough money to the public or private regime to receive benefits
- Pension Contribution Subsidy Program, which subsidizes contributions to the pension system for a range of groups—low-income workers, including the self-employed, people with disabilities, the unemployed, surrogate mothers, and councilors of small municipalities. The beneficiaries must contribute a percentage of the total contribution amount, which generally ranges between 5 percent and 30 percent, depending on the population group to which they belong. The remaining percentage is subsidized by the national government

Coverage of financial protection programs for old age is very low. Only 25 percent of the elderly population is covered by a pension, including the *Colombia Mayor* program, which benefits 1.6 million persons, the Periodic Economic Benefits Program, which benefits 578,000 people, and the Pension Contribution Subsidy Program, which benefits 155,000. Approximately 40 percent of the elderly population in Colombia are not covered by any transfer or social assistance program (Ministry of Health and Social Protection 2022).

Regarding the private sector, the programs carried out by the Family Compensation Funds[6] provide social services, such as loans, recreation, tourism, and sports, to the elderly. These programs benefit primarily workers or family members of formal employees (70 percent), with pensioners accounting for only 22 percent.

Lack of a pension or some other financial protection mechanism obliges some older people to remain in the labor market despite reaching retirement age. The elderly population represents approximately 10 percent of the employed population nationwide. A significant percentage of this population—66 percent—receive the minimum wage or less, 18 percent receive up to two times the minimum wage, 4.9 percent receive up to three times the minimum wage, and 7 percent receive more than three times the minimum wage, so the ability to accumulate savings is limited (Ministry of Health and Social Protection 2022).

Although Colombia has created various programs and sources of financing for elderly care, they are insufficient to meet the needs of this

---

BOX 2.1 Model of Care in Bogotá: Implementation of the District Care System

Providing care in an unbalanced manner limits women's access to the labor market, political participation, and ability to lead a life free of violence. One structural cause of this inequality is the gendered division of labor, which forces millions of women to carry out unpaid care work within the home. This overload of low-appreciation care work worsens the quality of life of many women and generates poverty of time, hindering the possibility of enjoying their rights to work, education, health, culture, and recreation.

In Bogotá, 9 of 10 women perform domestic and care work, particularly for the elderly, without any remuneration. On average, they spend 5 hours 33 minutes per day doing unpaid domestic and care work (DANE 2017).

Since May 2020, Bogotá has implemented a model of care that is provided by unpaid women and is aimed at people who require care according to their level of dependency. It was developed in the 20 locations that make up the district and is based on the monitoring system for the programs, projects, and goals of the Development Plan of Bogotá DC 2020–2024. It served 122,302 elderly people in 2020 and 156,727 in 2021.

This model of care has three operating strategies: (a) care neighbor blocks, in which people under care are assigned to specific caregivers and interdisciplinary groups; (b) mobile units, which reach out to the vulnerable population and caregivers in rural and peripheral areas; and (c) house-to-house care, which provides care to people who cannot access either of the other strategies. The model requires a comprehensive evaluation so that it can be incorporated as a national policy and then scaled to other territorial entities.

Source: Departamento Nacional de Planeación 2020.

---

vulnerable population. Many of the resources are allocated in the National Development Plan, and some are allocated through the territorial entities. Additionally, the resources collected from the stamp tax for older adults[7] are too meager, and the mechanisms for monitoring the collection and application of these resources are inadequate.

Since October 2020, Bogotá has been implementing a new program of care for the elderly. This program takes an inclusive gender and feminist approach that addresses both the elderly population and their caregivers (box 2.1).

Challenges

Reducing social inequalities for this vulnerable population group is an ethical imperative that the government and society must resolve together.

Increases in life expectancy and noncommunicable diseases have placed aging squarely on the international public policy agenda, posing challenges to social protection and public health. Besides the other formidable tasks they already face, country health systems need to address a growing elderly population that presents with multiple morbidities, which often carry high costs for health systems (Berrío Valencia 2012).

In this regard, the establishment of health care arrangements that cater to the complex needs of the elderly may require not only fundamental reforms in the way the entire health care system is organized and care is delivered, but also a reconsideration of the social determinants that affect health outcomes. For example, the PHC model is emerging as a strategy to facilitate the objectives of Colombia's policy on aging and old age: to ensure that older adults can enjoy this stage of their life with autonomy, dignity, and a sense of inclusion, within a framework that restores, protects, promotes, and fully realizes their human rights (Ministry of Health and Social Protection 2015). These objectives also align with the purposes of the Ten-Year Public Health Plan 2022–2031 (Ministry of Health and Social Protection 2023), which recognizes the integral role of primary health care. Other important challenges include the following:

- Training health care workers in gerontology and geriatrics and offering them work, especially at the subnational level in rural and remote areas.

- Strengthening the processes of economic security in old age and intergenerational solidarity to create an inclusive society for all ages that does not tolerate any form of age discrimination.

- Strengthening intersectoral collaboration between the health sector, territorial entities, and the private sector to promote the protection of old age and healthy aging, which includes expanding the Family Compensation Funds to increase the coverage of social programs.

- Strengthening coordination between the leading public sectors responsible for health and social programs, particularly at the territory level, to support the elderly—especially those who are functionally dependent on others for care—in a holistic way.

- Guaranteeing the financial sustainability of actions proposed by the National Public Policy on Aging and Old Age.

- Reducing inequities in both access to and use of new information and communication technologies by the elderly, especially the hearing and visually impaired, in order to close the digital gap for this population, which entails designing and financing training programs for older adults in the use of these technologies.

- Establishing mechanisms to monitor the circumstances of the elderly population through periodic surveys such as SABE (the last such survey was in 2015).

- Improving the coverage of the Colombian pension system for the elderly, especially for those who, during their career, worked in the informal economic sector. Not only has the general pension system not extended coverage to the elderly, but its current guidelines and the presence of a high percentage of labor informality could even worsen the situation in the coming years (Fedesarrollo and Saldarriaga Concha Foundation 2015).

- Guaranteeing the right to healthy aging, the right to decent work, and the right to equal opportunities and treatment. Many older adults wish to continue working and living productively beyond retirement age, but for this to happen, the government and society as a whole need to ensure compliance with certain requirements; in particular, they must guarantee that the work older people do is developed under legal and ethical parameters and that it meets conditions that promote their functionality, sense of competence, health, and well-being. Urgently needed is an examination of issues such as labor informality, which is prevalent among this population and not only violates the right to social security but also robs individuals of the possibility of enjoying good working conditions, health, and the safety and stability they need for continuing their career.

Recommendations

- *Strengthen institutional capacity to develop the National Public Policy on Aging and Old Age 2022–2031 and formulate its National Intersectoral Action Plan.* In particular, implementation of the policy should be monitored and evaluated through the National Observatory on Aging and Old Age, in coordination with other observatories such as the National Health Observatory, the National Institute of Health, and the Observatory of Violence of the National Institute of Legal Medicine and Forensic Sciences.

- *Strengthen health care through the development of guidelines and care protocols.* Such protocols need to address geriatric syndromes and multiple morbidity in an interdisciplinary manner from the perspective of humanized care centered on older persons and their abilities.

- *Develop and implement age-friendly care centers.* These centers need to consider the limitations that many older people in Colombia have in terms of low educational attainment and difficulties in accessing and using information and computer technology.

- *Promote the development of the main pillars of the National Public Policy on Aging and Old Age 2022–2031.* These strategic pillars include (a) helping older adults to overcome their economic dependence; (b) fostering the social inclusion and citizen participation of older adults; (c) achieving a violence-free life for older adults; (d) providing comprehensive health care, dependency care, and organization of care services; (e) supporting healthy aging to maintain an independent, autonomous, and productive life in old age; and (f) financing education, training, and research to meet the challenges of aging and old age.

Notes

1. The 2015 SABE focused on the elderly population. It was the first survey in the Latin America and the Caribbean region to focus on the national level rather than exclusively on cities (Ministry of Health and Social Protection 2015).
2. An older person presents a disability condition when he or she needs help with at least one basic activity of daily living.
3. Socioeconomic stratification classifies residential properties that receive public utility services such as electricity, natural gas, water, and sewage services by their socioeconomic status. It is carried out mainly to charge residences in a differential manner for public services, allowing the allocation of subsidies and collection of contributions. Households with greater economic capacity thus pay more, and households with less economic capacity pay less (DANE n.d.).

4. In Colombia, people belonging to the contributory regime are those—together with their families—who have a formal employment contract, are self-employed workers with income capacity, or are pensioners. The subsidized regime sponsors health coverage for poor and vulnerable people who cannot pay and who are selected through a household survey that categorizes the population by socioeconomic status.

5. As of 2014, the unemployment protection mechanism, among other benefits, guarantees, for a maximum period of six months, the payment of pension contributions—determined on the basis of a minimum wage—to workers who lose their job (Law 1636 of 2013, on the mechanism of protection of the unemployed in Colombia).

6. The Family Compensation Funds are private, nonprofit entities committed to economic redistribution and solidarity. They were created to improve the quality of life of the families of Colombian workers through the management and delivery of subsidies and services from part of the social security contributions made by employers. Refer to Ospina (2021).

7. In Colombia, the stamp (*estampilla*) is a parafiscal tax that companies or individuals who sign contracts with public entities such as government departments must pay. The resources are earmarked for a specific sector and are intended to cover expenses incurred by entities that develop or provide public services. The resources collected by the "stamp for the well-being of the elderly" created by Law 1276 of 2009 are used to assist and care for the elderly in the departments.

References

Arrubla, Deisy Jeannette. 2014. *Vejez y asistencialismo en épocas neoliberales: Colombia 1970–2009*. Bogotá: Universidad Nacional de Colombia. http://www.bdigital.unal.edu.co/40973/1/598362.2014.pdf.

Berrío Valencia, Marta Inés. 2012. "Envejecimiento de la población: Un reto para la salud pública." *Colombian Journal of Anesthesiology* 40 (3): 192–94.

Colombian Truth Commission. 2022. *There Is a Future if There Is Truth. Final Report.* Bogotá: Colombian Truth Commission.

Corte Constitucional. 1991. *Constitución política de Colombia: Actualizada con los actos legislativos a 2015*. Bogotá: Imprenta Nacional. http://web.presidencia.gov.co/constitucion/index.pdf.

DANE (Departamento Administrativo Nacional de Estadística). 2022. *Proyecciones de población: Censo nacional de población y vivienda*. Bogotá: DANE. https://www.dane.gov.co/index.php/estadisticas-por-tema/demografia-y-poblacion/proyecciones-de-poblacion.

DANE (Departamento Administrativo Nacional de Estadística). 2017. *Encuesta nacional del uso del tiempo (ENUT), 2016–17*. Bogotá: DANE and Dirección de Metodología y Producción Estadística. https://microdatos.dane.gov.co/index.php/catalog/552/.

DANE (Departamento Administrativo Nacional de Estadística). 2024. "Boletín técnico." https://www.dane.gov.co/index.php/estadisticas-por-tema/mercado-laboral/empleo-informal-y-seguridad-social.

DANE (Departamento Administrativo Nacional de Estadística). n.d. "Estratificación socioeconómica para servicios públicos domiciliarios." *Servicios al ciudadano* (blog). https://www.dane.gov.co/index.php/servicios-al-ciudadano/servicios-informacion/estratificacion-socioeconomica#.

Departamento Nacional de Planeación. 2020. *Implementación del Sistema Distrital de Cuidado en Bogotá*. Bogotá: Departamento Nacional de Planeación. https://www.sdp.gov.co/sites/default/files/121_sdmj_2020110010282_7718_0.pdf.

Fedesarrollo and Fundación Saldarriaga Concha. 2015. *Misión Colombia envejece: Cifras, retos y recomendaciones.* Bogotá: Editorial Fundación Saldarriaga Concha. https://www .repository.fedesarrollo.org.co/bitstream/handle/11445/2724/LIB_2015_MCE _completo.pdf?sequence=5&isAllowed=y.

Fleck, Anna. 2022. "How Many Victims Has Colombia's Armed Conflict Claimed?" *Statista,* July 12, 2022. https://www.statista.com/chart/27758/colombia-armed -conflict-number-of-victims.

Ministry of Health and Social Protection. 2015. *Estudio Nacional de Salud, Bienestar y Envejecimiento (SABE) Colombia 2015: Resumen ejecutivo.* Bogotá: Ministry of Health and Social Protection. https://www.minsalud.gov.co/sites/rid/Lists/BibliotecaDigital /RIDE/VS/ED/GCFI/Resumen-Ejecutivo-Encuesta-SABE.pdf.

Ministry of Health and Social Protection. 2017. "Resolución 024 de 2017." Ministry of Health and Social Protection, Bogotá. https://minsalud.gov.co/Normatividad_Nuevo /Resolución 0024 de 2017.pdf.

Ministry of Health and Social Protection. 2018. "Resolución 055 de 2018." Ministry of Health and Social Protection, Bogotá. https://www.minsalud.gov.co/sites/rid/Lists /BibliotecaDigital/RIDE/DE/DIJ/Resolucion-055-de-2018.pdf.

Ministry of Health and Social Protection. 2021a. *Análisis de situación de salud (ASIS).* Bogotá: Dirección de Epidemiología y Demografía, Ministry of Health and Social Protection. https://www.minsalud.gov.co/sites/rid/Lists/BibliotecaDigital/RIDE/VS /ED/PSP/analisis-situacion-salud-colombia-2021.pdf.

Ministry of Health and Social Protection. 2021b. "Plantilla 3-4 Pirámide poblacional: Índices demográficos." Ministry of Health and Social Protection, Bogotá. https:// www.minsalud.gov.co/sites/rid/lists/bibliotecadigital/ride/vs/ed/psp/plantilla_3-4 _piramide_poblacional.pdf.

Ministry of Health and Social Protection. 2022. "Decreto 681 de 2022." Ministry of Health and Social Protection, Bogotá. https://www.minsalud.gov.co/Normatividad _Nuevo/Decreto No. 681 de 2022.pdf.

Ministry of Health and Social Protection. 2023. "Resolución 2367 de 2023." Ministry of Health and Social Protection, Bogotá. https://www.minsalud.gov.co/Normatividad _Nuevo/Resolución No 2367 de 2023.pdf.

Ministry of Health and Social Protection and Profamilia. 2015. *Encuesta nacional de demografía y salud.* Vol. 1. Bogotá: Ministry of Health and Social Protection. https://dhsprogram.com/:pubs/pdf/fr334/fr334.pdf.

Ospina, Juan Carlos. 2021. "Qué son las Cajas de Compensación Familiar y para qué sirven." *Rankia* (pensions blog), October 10, 2021. https://www.rankia.co/blog/pen siones-iss-cesantias/3233802-que-son-cajas-compensacion-familiar-para-sirven.

Parra, Julian A., Fernando Arias, Jesus Bejarano, Martha López, Juan Ospina, Julio Romero, and Eduardo Sarmiento. 2020. "Sistema pensional colombiano: Descripción, tendencias demográficas y análisis macroeconómico." *Ensayos Sobre Política Económica* 96: 1–64. https://doi.org/10.32468/espe.96.

Peñaloza, Rolando, Natalia Salamanca, Jorge Rodríguez, Jesus Rodríguez, and Andrés Beltrán. 2014. *Estimación de la carga de enfermedad para Colombia, 2010,* 1st ed. Bogotá: Editorial Pontificia Universidad Javeriana. https://repository.javeriana.edu .co/bitstream/handle/10554/40972/9789587166996.pdf?sequence=3&isAllowed=y.

CHAPTER 3

Mongolia: Meeting Older Adults' Health Needs through PHC and Getting the Most from Screening Programs

Tumurbat Byamba, Evlegsuren Ser-Od, Khishgee Majigzav, Enkhjargal Altangerel, Tsolmongerel Tsilaajav, Naranzul Nyamsuren, Unurmaa Enebish, Nandintsetseg Tsoggerel, Tsogzolmaa Khurelerdene, Pagma Genden, Kate Mandeville, Vikram Rajan, and Xiaohui Hou

Key Messages

- Mongolia's population ages 60 and older is growing steadily, and almost half of Mongolians ages 45–69 are at high risk of developing a noncommunicable disease (NCD).
- Mongolia has sought to integrate primary health care (PHC) and social welfare services to address challenges such as the cost of medications and transportation for older adults seeking health services and rehabilitative care. However, Mongolia's PHC centers generally lack the tools and strategies needed to prevent chronic diseases and promote healthy aging. PHC services for older adults are largely reactive (curative).
- Opportunities exist to strengthen Mongolia's disease screening programs. Using financing and administrative measures to shift screening progressively from hospitals to PHC facilities could reduce workloads at referral hospitals and boost system efficiency.

Background

The population of Mongolia is still relatively young, but the number of older adults—defined as persons ages 60 or older—has been growing steadily. In 2021, Mongolia had a population of about 3.4 million, of which 262,265 (7.7 percent) were ages 60 and older, with more women than men in this age group. Policies addressing Mongolia's longer life expectancy and consequent

FIGURE 3.1 Age Pyramid of Mongolia, 2021

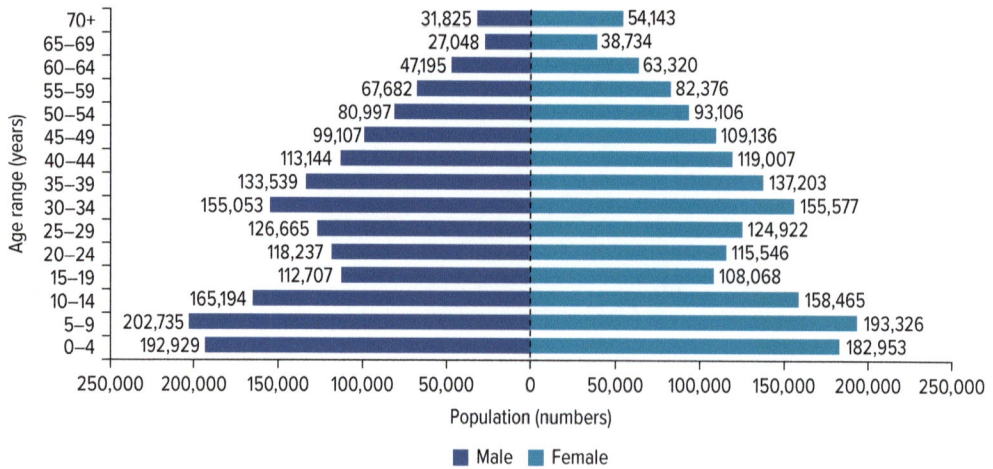

Source: Center for Health Development 2022.

increase in the elderly population are needed to provide a sustainable system for healthy aging. People ages 30–44 constitute the second-largest segment of the population. The government needs to begin planning now for when these adults enter their later years and begin to require health care geared toward the elderly (figure 3.1).

The prevalence of common NCD risk factors is high in older Mongolian adults. Almost half of individuals ages 45–69 are at high risk of developing a noncommunicable disease, with men 1.5 times more likely than women. Currently, 73.7 percent of the population ages 55–69 regularly take medicine for hypertension, 13.7 percent have confirmed diabetes, 22.7 percent have high morning blood sugar levels, and 38.3 percent have high triglyceride levels. Cardiovascular disease is a reality for 19.3 percent of the population, and more than 30 percent are at risk of developing it in the coming 10 years.

Individuals ages 60 and older account for 56.2 percent of all deaths in Mongolia. Cardiovascular, respiratory, and gastrointestinal diseases, cancer, and injuries are the leading causes of death in this age group. The STEPS (STEPwise approach to noncommunicable disease risk factor surveillance) Survey in 2020 revealed potential focus areas for health care interventions relating to nicotine, diet, and exercise (Ministry of Health 2020a).

In 2016, one-quarter of the Mongolian elderly population were found to be moderately or significantly dependent on others for the performance of basic daily activities, with women more likely to need help than men. Five percent of older adults were categorized as having severe cognitive impairment (Asian Development Bank 2020). Given the inevitability of aging and the compounding effects of ill health, proactive interventions to maintain good health become more important as a nation's older population grows in size.

The Case Study Methodology

This country case study provides information on Mongolia's PHC-centered integrated care system for older adults using the financing, innovation, regulation, and evaluation (FIRE) framework. It also qualitatively assesses the implementation of an adult screening program and identifies further development needs.

A desk review of legal and policy documents related to aging care was conducted, along with an analysis of secondary data (health statistics) on service use by older adults and select health indicators disaggregated according to age and sex. A comprehensive review of an adult screening program's technical documents was carried out to assess the development of population-based screening services in Mongolia, and a cross-sectional qualitative study was carried out to determine the performance of the current screening program. The technical guidelines were compared to arrive at a thorough understanding of how the adult screening program evolved in Mongolia. Responses were sorted according to the FIRE framework, and a descriptive analysis was performed to identify recurrent themes and patterns in the data.

Case Study Findings

Overview of Aging Care in PHC

In 2016, the Mongolian Parliament passed a resolution to approve the Mongolian Sustainable Development Concept—2030, aligned to support the United Nation's Sustainable Development Goals. The concept provided a road map divided into three periods (figure 3.2), with specific goals to support the overarching objective of increasing life expectancy to 78 years by 2030.

FIGURE 3.2 Mongolian Sustainable Development Concept—2030

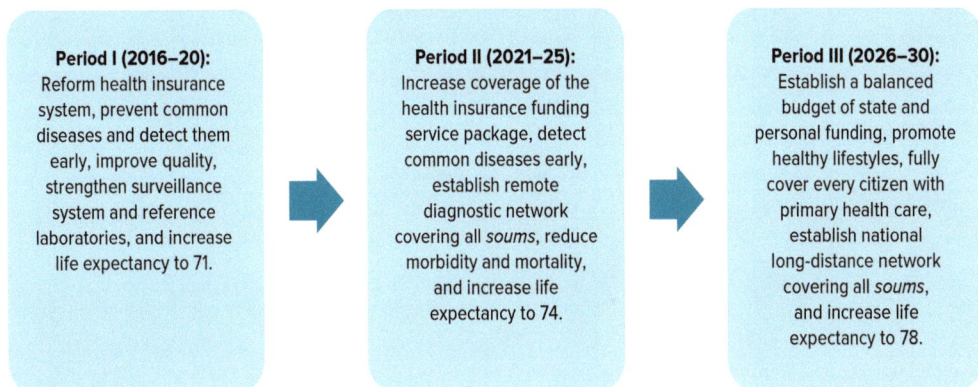

Period I (2016–20):
Reform health insurance system, prevent common diseases and detect them early, improve quality, strengthen surveillance system and reference laboratories, and increase life expectancy to 71.

Period II (2021–25):
Increase coverage of the health insurance funding service package, detect common diseases early, establish remote diagnostic network covering all *soums*, reduce morbidity and mortality, and increase life expectancy to 74.

Period III (2026–30):
Establish a balanced budget of state and personal funding, promote healthy lifestyles, fully cover every citizen with primary health care, establish national long-distance network covering all *soums*, and increase life expectancy to 78.

Source: Secretariat of the State Great Hural 2016.

Regulation of PHC Services

In Mongolia, the provision of health care to older adults is regulated by state laws, government resolutions, and orders of cabinet members (the ministers of health and of social welfare). The Mongolian Constitution and six additional laws that are specific to health care for the general population and for older adults outline the fundamental legal requirements for health care provision in Mongolia (table 3.1). These laws include support measures such as counseling and training for older adults, reimbursement of voucher costs, and transportation for treatment, monitoring, discounted medicines, and the provision of prosthetic limbs and devices for hearing, sight, and mobility.

Innovations in Service Delivery: Integration of Care for Older Adults into PHC

PHC facilities are an individual's first point of contact with the health care system. They provide a bundle of essential services, including health promotion, illness prevention, treatment, rehabilitation, and palliative care. The Health Law of Mongolia 2011 defines PHC services as family health care services and essential care services provided to each person in the territory, with the participation of citizens, families, and business entities, based on the health care needs of the population (Government of Mongolia 2011).

Two types of facilities provide primary health care: family health centers (FHCs) and *soum* (administrative subdivision) health centers (SHCs). The FHC

TABLE 3.1 Documents Regulating the Provision of Care to Older Adults at PHC Centers in Mongolia

Legal environment	Documents
Regulation for service provision	• Family health center operating rule, approved by Health Minister Order No. A/04 of 2017 • Package service of *soum* and village health center, approved by Health Minister Order No. A/52 of 2019 • Guideline for clinical management for older adults, approved by Health Minister Order No. A/517 of 2019 • Procedure for rehabilitation management and day care, approved by Health Minister Order No. A/502 of 2019
Innovations in service delivery	• Procedure for referring to upper-level health care facilities, approved by Health Minister Order No. A/256 of 2018 • Procedure for referring to rehabilitation center, approved by Health Minister Order No. A/247 of 2012
Funding	• Procedure for reimbursement amount, payment method, and regulation, Resolution by National Committee for Health Insurance 05, of 2022 • Procedure for quality control of medical care and payment regulation, Resolution by National Committee for Health Insurance 05, of 2021
Evaluation	• Family health center performance agreement model, approved by Health Minister Order No. A/05 of 2017 • Procedure for health statistics, reporting, and analysis, approved by Health Minister Order No. A/611 of 2019

Source: Compilation of documents on the Ministry of Health official website (https://www.moh.gov.mn).

structure and staffing model is similar to that of PHC providers in other countries, but the SHC structure is unique to Mongolia.

The rural population of Mongolia is scattered across a vast land area; *soum* health centers provide primary health care and are equipped with hospital beds to provide inpatient hospital services. Family health centers were introduced in Mongolia in 1999 in the form of family group practice, which is a partnership of private general practitioners who provide health services to households and ensure affordable universal access to basic health services for all Mongolian citizens, including older adults.

As of 2021, 208 family health centers and 321 *soum* health centers were providing PHC services. In Mongolia's capital city, Ulaanbaatar, 131 family health centers provide PHC services for 1.7 million inhabitants. The 728,400 people living in Mongolia's 21 *aimag* (tribal) centers are supported by 77 family health centers. Table 3.2 compares the availability and use of select services in family and *soum* health centers, by location.

Mongolia has an estimated 1.9 to 2.3 times as many doctors per 10,000 population working in *soum* health centers as in family health centers in urban settings (Ulaanbaatar and *aimag* centers). The doctor-nurse ratio is 1:1 in family health centers and 1:2 in *soum* health centers. Each family health center in Ulaanbaatar provides health care to an average of 13,000 people, and each *aimag* family health center provides care to an average of 10,000 people. Each *soum* health center provides care to an average of 3,100 people, which is 25–30 percent fewer than other health centers.

Mongolia's population has been migrating from rural to urban areas, but the number of SHC doctors has remained static, causing an inequality in access to primary health care (WHO 2013). The number of PHC facilities has not changed or, in some places has decreased, as the population has grown in urban areas.

The average number of outpatient examinations per doctor per working day is about 18 in the Ulaanbaatar family health centers, 22 in *aimag* family health centers, and 11 in *soum* health centers. *Soum* doctors perform half as many examinations as *aimag* doctors, due in part to the small size of the *soum* population

TABLE 3.2 Availability and Use Indicators for Family and *Soum* Health Centers in Mongolia, 2021

Indicator	Family health centers		*Soum* health centers
	Ulaanbaatar	*Aimag* centers	
Number of facilities	131	77	321
Number of doctors per 10,000 population	4.3	5.1	9.9
Number of nurses per 10,000 population	8.9	4.9	18.5
Number of people per primary health care facility	12,993	9,916	3,121
Ratio of doctor to nurses	1:1	1:1	1:2
Number of examinations per doctor per year	4,518.2	5,520.3	2,946.4
Average number of examinations per doctor per day	17.7	21.6	11.5

Source: Center for Health Development 2022.
Note: Aimag = province; *Soum* = secondary administrative subdivision.

and to the accessibility of *soum* health centers. According to an interview participant,

> Nomadic people live far and do not come to the health center unless they have a serious health problem, so we must organize a trip for them and provide basic services such as regular check-ups or screening. The main thing is that it takes a lot of time, so we make our own plan and schedule and do the examinations and tests. The shortage of human resources and equipment is a big concern.

The Mongolian public health system outlines an approach for proactive health care and follow-up services at family and *soum* health centers. Ideally, health care providers at both types of centers should assess the health of the people within their catchment area based on established criteria ranging from individuals in good health to persons with established health conditions requiring active monitoring and follow-up care.

Basic medical services—including diagnostics, treatment, emergency care, palliative care, rehabilitation services, nursing care, home care, day care, and traditional medical care—are part of primary health care. PHC centers should provide the following public health services: health education, vaccination, screening for common noncommunicable diseases, surveillance of infectious diseases, promotion of rational drug use, and collection of health service data.

Specific to health care provision for older adults, PHC facilities provide health monitoring to improve quality of life, care for bedridden older people and people with disabilities, and care for older adults who need welfare care. Services are provided in accordance with Mongolia's clinical diagnostic and management guidelines (table 3.3).

In addition, the Mongolian health system has outlined the following targeted health services for older adults through PHC facilities (Government of Mongolia 2017a):

- One or two preventive visits per year
- Referrals to hospital or rehabilitation care
- Monthly home visit
- Regular home visits for bedridden older adults and those with disabilities
- Advice on age-appropriate physical activities
- Active monitoring of health status.

TABLE 3.3 Services for Older Adults at PHC Facilities in Mongolia

Service	Prevention	Diagnosis	Treatment	Monitor	Referral
Monitoring of health status	+	+	+	+	+
Care for bedridden older adults and adults with disabilities	+	+	+	+	+
Care for older adults in need of welfare	+	+	+	+	+

Source: Health Minister Order A/129, 2017 (Ministry of Health 2017).
Note: + = required; PHC = primary health care.

This approach to providing robust health services for aging adults is a step in the right direction. However, limited capacity at health facilities, coupled with high caseloads, significantly limits the implementation of the recommended public health measures.

Integration of Primary Health Care with Referral Level of Care

A well-organized referral system is an important function of comprehensive, integrated health care, and Mongolia's referral system is still developing. The procedure for referral to upper-level health care facilities was approved by Health Minister Order No. A256 of 2018, which regulates the integration of the services of primary and referral facilities (except emergency care) (figure 3.3).

1. PHC facilities refer patients to *aimag* and district general hospitals, district health centers, maternity hospitals, private hospitals, and clinics in accordance with instructions for diagnosis and treatment.

2. *Aimag* and district general hospitals, health centers, maternity hospitals, and private health organizations refer patients to specialized hospitals.

3. PHC facilities refer patients directly to specialized hospitals and centers if they have been diagnosed previously, have required repeated treatment, are located far from the *aimag* hospital, or require urgent transfer.

4. The receiving health care facility establishes a connection with the referring provider.

FIGURE 3.3 Referral Procedure in Mongolia's Health System

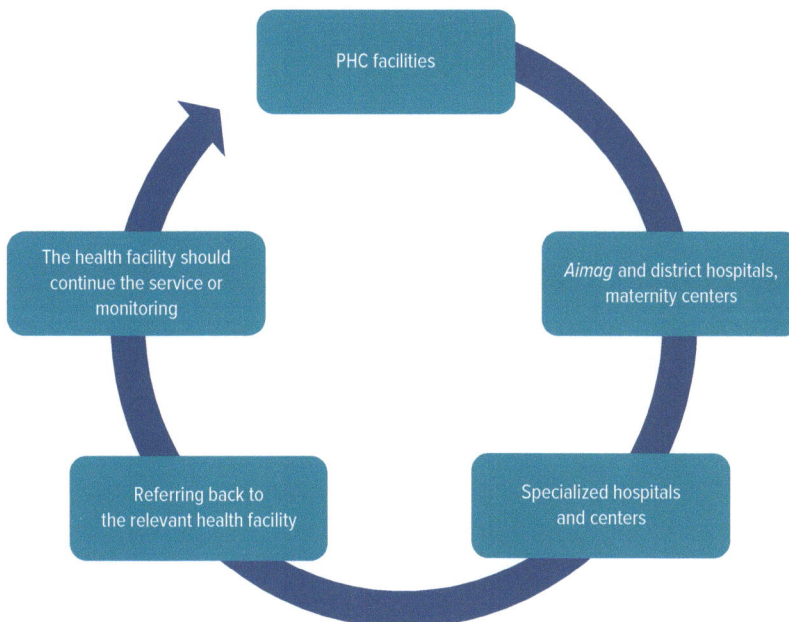

Source: Health Minister Order No. A256, 2018 (Ministry of Health 2018).
Note: Aimag = province; PHC = primary health care.

5. The receiving health care facility provides the required services at the scheduled time.

6. After treatment, the receiving health care facility sends the patient back to the referring health facility for continued monitoring and advice to ensure continuity of care.

Referrals are made in both paper and electronic format, and both are accepted as valid. Family and *soum* health centers complete Registration Form AM-13, "Patient Referral Form," and then transfer the patient. The appointment date and time are scheduled via telephone or email.

Electronic referrals are made in the web-based H-info system and in other systems that the health care facilities use. The system has four main menus: refer, appointment, accept, and feedback to referrer (figure 3.4). Regulations for integrating the levels of health care are well documented and implemented.

Integration of PHC and Social Welfare Services for Older Adults

PHC facilities provide four services in close collaboration with the social welfare sector to support older adults in accordance with Government of Mongolia Resolution 197 of 2017 (Government of Mongolia 2017b):

- *Prosthesis cost reimbursement.* The Mongolian Social Welfare Fund and the Health Insurance Fund provide reimbursement for limb prostheses, orthopedic devices for hearing and vision impairments, wheelchairs, and dentures purchased by or made for older adults with a prescription.

- *Medicine cost subsidization.* The Health Insurance Fund offsets the cost of medication for older adults by subsidizing the Health Insurance General Office's approved list of essential medicines. Older adults can purchase subsidized medicines with a prescription from an FHC or SHC doctor.

- *Transport cost reimbursement for older adults living in remote areas.* The cost of a one-way trip (half of the total trip cost) is eligible for reimbursement once a year for older adults who live more than 1,000 kilometers from the capital and are referred to a specialized hospital. Receiving hospitals are required to provide any necessary medical services without delay.

FIGURE 3.4   Electronic Referral Procedure between Health Care Facilities in Mongolia

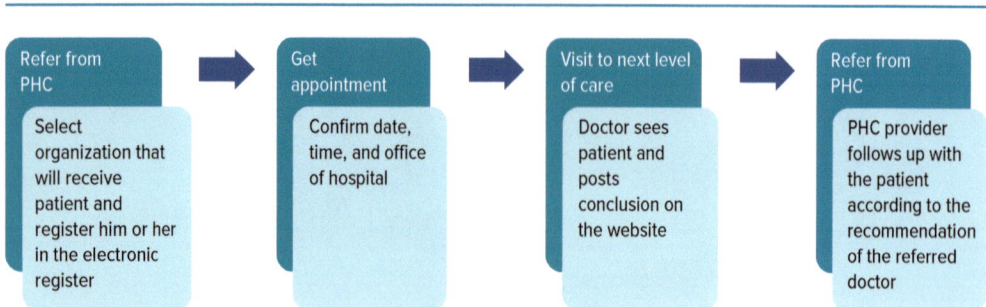

Refer from PHC		Get appointment		Visit to next level of care		Refer from PHC
Select organization that will receive patient and register him or her in the electronic register	→	Confirm date, time, and office of hospital	→	Doctor sees patient and posts conclusion on the website	→	PHC provider follows up with the patient according to the recommendation of the referred doctor

Source: Health Minister Order No. A256, 2018 (Ministry of Health 2018).
Note: PHC = primary health care.

- *Rehabilitation cost subsidization.* The Social Welfare Fund offsets the cost of rehabilitation services for older adults at accredited facilities. Half of the cost of rehabilitation services in an accredited facility is paid for by the Social Welfare Fund upon presentation of a referral form issued by an FHC or SHC physician. Patients are also eligible for reimbursement of half of their transportation costs.

Government Resolution No. 197 also recommends the following actions:

- Collaborate between sectors to build an environment in which older adults can meet their basic needs and have an adequate standard of living, learn, grow, make decisions, be mobile, build and maintain relationships, and contribute to society
- Conduct assessments to identify both unhelpful and constructive (traditional and modern) attitudes toward age and aging, common types of ageism, and discrimination against older adults to generate evidence that can inform policy actions under the "combating ageism" action area
- Transform health services into integrated, person-centered, gender-sensitive, and age-friendly services
- Provide essential health care services that meet the actual health needs of older adults by revamping the bundle of PHC services and allocating adequate funding to support service provision
- Increase the number of organizations providing long-term sanatorium, rehabilitation, and palliative care services through government policies
- Establish community-based centers in *soums*, districts, and *khoroos* (subdistricts of Ulaanbaatar) to reduce the social isolation of older adults and to promote their mental, psychological, and emotional health
- Include person-centered, elder-friendly indicators of access to good-quality care in the evaluation criteria for organizations that provide PHC services.

With regard to screening services, the following actions are recommended:

- Evaluate the efficacy and cost-effectiveness of the current screening program and update the bundles based on the assessment
- Implement financial and administrative mechanisms to increase the participation of PHC facilities in delivering screening services to balance the workload of referral-level hospitals, whose primary responsibility is to diagnose and treat patients, not to detect suspected cases
- Make more funding available for screening programs so that every adult can be screened every year and organize screening with optimal frequency based on actual health risks to increase funding per person and reduce the cost of detecting one case
- Prioritize routine technical and administrative guidance and coordination with health organizations along with regular trainings to ensure the smooth implementation of screening

- Regularly update technical documents, such as clinical guidelines and diagnostic procedures used for screening, and translate them into Mongolian using internationally accepted tools
- Promote the importance of screening among the general population by providing information about how, where, for what, and when to be screened and inform the public about the expected results and benefits of screening.

Financing of PHC and Geriatric Care

PHC services are free and funded from the state budget and the Health Insurance Fund. Capitation payment is the main form of funding for essential services provided at the PHC facilities. The population is divided into five groups, based on age and health risks. Each group is divided into two subgroups by type of housing: either traditional housing in a *ger* (a circular canvas and felt tent with limited sanitation facilities used by Mongolian nomads) or a modern apartment. This model results in 10 rates for calculating per capita funding for each PHC facility.

Around 2012, the government determined that per capita rates were too low and should be raised. Government resolutions were passed between 2012 and 2021 to increase the rates for each age group (table 3.4). In 2022, the highest rate was for children under 5, which was 3.5 times higher than in 2018. The second-highest rate was for essential care for adults ages 60 and older.

In accordance with Article 9.1.9 of the Law on Health Insurance, PHC facilities, in addition to per capita funding for basic health services, must provide four other types of health services: diagnostic procedures, home care, rehabilitation, and day treatment (Government of Mongolia 2015). The cost of these services is reimbursed according to case-based claims submitted to the Health Insurance Fund. Table 3.5 presents the latest rate for case-based payment for the additional services.

TABLE 3.4 Per Capita Rate for PHC Facilities in Mongolia, 2018–22

Age (years)	Housing condition	Health risk coefficient	Risk-based per capita payment rate (tughriks)				
			2018	2019	2020	2021	2022
Under 5	*Ger* area	3.0	30,420	30,420	53,316	53,316	106,632
	Apartment	2.6	26,364	26,364	46,207	46,207	92,414
6–15	*Ger* area	1.3	13,182	13,182	23,104	23,104	46,208
	Apartment	1.2	12,168	12,168	21,326	21,326	42,652
Women, 16–49	*Ger* area	1.4	14,196	14,196	24,881	24,881	49,762
	Apartment	1.4	14,196	14,196	24,881	24,881	49,762
60 and older	*Ger* area	**1.9**	**19,266**	**19,266**	**33,767**	**33,767**	**67,534**
	Apartment	**1.7**	**17,238**	**17,238**	**30,212**	**30,212**	**60,424**
Other	*Ger* area	1.1	11,154	11,154	19,549	19,549	39,098
	Apartment	1.0	10,140	10,140	17,772	17,772	35,544

Source: National Health Insurance Board 2022.
Note: A *ger* is a circular canvas and felt tent with limited sanitation facilities used by Mongolian nomads.

TABLE 3.5 Case-Based Payment Rate from the Health Insurance Fund to PHC Facilities in Mongolia, 2022

Type of treatment	Payment rate (tughriks)
Diagnostic procedures	20,000
Home care	70,000
Rehabilitation	45,000
Day treatment	70,000

Source: National Health Insurance Board 2019.
Note: PHC = primary health care.

TABLE 3.6 Claims Submitted to the Health Insurance Fund for the Four Types of Services Provided at PHC Facilities and Reimbursement in Mongolia, 2021

Type of service	Claims		Reimbursement	
	Number	%	Amount (tughriks, million)	%
Home care	60,995	13.7	5,644.2	37.4
Diagnostic procedures	258,173	58.1	2,693.9	17.8
Day treatment	61,840	13.9	4,235.2	28.0
Rehabilitation services	63,366	14.3	2,542.6	16.8
Total	444,374	100.0	15,135.9	100.0

Source: Health Insurance General Office 2021.
Note: PHC = primary health care.

In 2021, the Health Insurance General Office transferred Tog 15.1 billion (tughriks) to cover 444,374 claims submitted by PHC facilities for the four types of services. Although diagnostic procedures represent 58.1 percent of total claims, home care receives the most funding, representing 37.4 percent of total reimbursement payments (table 3.6).

Disaggregation of claims according to age group reveals that 37.1 percent of claims are for services delivered to individuals ages 60 and older, indicating the importance of PHC services for older adults.

Monitoring and Evaluation of PHC

Access to, quality of, and operation of primary health care are monitored and evaluated by analyzing health management information systems, conducting on-site assessments, evaluating contract performance with the Health Insurance Agency, assessing the performance of family health centers, and conducting audits through specialized inspection agencies.

Every type of organization that provides PHC services must report on required indicators and information within the framework of health management information. The required information includes population morbidity and mortality; maternal and child mortality; and indicators of daily, monthly, quarterly, and annual outpatient and inpatient care. The collected data reflect the

TABLE 3.7 Accreditation Criteria for Services for Older Adults at PHC Facilities in Mongolia

Criteria	Family health centers	*Soum* health centers
At least 80% of older adults have been screened	+	+
Older, bedridden adults with disabilities are 100% supported and provided with care at home	+	+
Home care and service records are kept	+	+
Guidance and counseling are provided to caregivers of older adults	+	+
Reports and analysis are undertaken	+	—

Source: Ministry of Health 2020b.
Note: PHC = primary health care; *Soum* = secondary administrative subdivision; + = required; — = not required.

current status, availability, and quality of health care resources and services and also provide evidence for future policy and planning.

The quality of PHC services is monitored and ensured through accreditation of the family and *soum* health centers. Some of the criteria for accreditation pertain specifically to services for older adults, including coverage rates for preventive examinations, service rates for bedridden and disabled older adults, home care, and training for caregivers (table 3.7). Accreditation is granted for three to five years, depending on service quality performance. All PHC facilities must be accredited to obtain Health Insurance Fund payments.

All licensed and accredited health facilities contract with the Health Insurance General Office to obtain funding for the services provided. In turn, the Health Insurance General Office monitors and evaluates patient orientation and the quality, effectiveness, and efficiency of the services provided.

A performance agreement exists between the family health center, the *aimag* or city governor's office, and the health department. Performance indicators for older adults in family health centers are assessed annually.

The following three indicators are related to the care provided to older adults at family health centers:

1. Annual update of the registration of older adults in the catchment area

2. Preventive care examination coverage rate for older adults

3. Percentage of elderly people who engage regularly in age-appropriate exercise.

In rural areas, *soum* health centers are evaluated against structural and operational standards according to the following criteria:

• At least 70 percent of older adults have undergone routine screening

• Bedridden and vulnerable older adults with disabilities are monitored regularly

• Home, day care, and rehabilitation services are covered for older adults.

Monitoring and evaluation of service provision for older adults is included in the overall performance assessment of PHC facilities.

Conclusions and Lessons

Public health activities at PHC facilities include health promotion, health education, disease prevention, early detection, health monitoring, rehabilitation, counseling, social protection, welfare, and community-based care. However, because of a lack of human resources for primary care services, the heavy workload in these facilities, and financial constraints, public health care is not well implemented at PHC facilities. Specific to older adults, the services at PHC facilities are mostly after-the-fact reactive rather than proactive measures aimed at promoting healthy aging and maintaining the functional abilities and intrinsic capacities of older adults. In general, PHC facilities lack services designed to maintain and improve older people's basic functional abilities and intrinsic capacities, including locomotor, sensory (hearing and eyesight), cognitive, and psychological competencies.

Because of their unique situation and role, *soum* health centers focus more on medical care than on the other essential PHC services, including geriatric care. Family health centers' efforts to provide comprehensive social and health care for older adults are also limited by the large catchment areas they serve and health care needs of the diverse populations within them.

Since 2012, population screening based on age, sex, and health risks has been developing gradually in Mongolia. If it is implemented in a sustainable way, with continued improvements, the screening program is expected to reduce mortality, extend life expectancy, and facilitate healthy aging. Screening for hearing, vision, dental, and locomotor disorders that are specific to older adults and involve less expensive procedures is necessary to care for an aging population. The reintroduction of these screenings should be considered thoroughly based on evidence generated from data analysis, desk reviews, and needs assessments. The current screening bundle raises concerns about the frequency, targets, and overall cost-effectiveness of the bundle and approach. More screening does not necessarily equate to better outcomes.

The importance of PHC facilities in implementing screening programs should not be overlooked, and specialized centers at the top of the medical care pyramid should not be overburdened with screening procedures. However, the latest screening regulations are not consistent with these principles. Overall, changing the regulations frequently is not advisable because each change imposes a learning curve and may be experienced as disruptive and unsettling because it entails a range of institutional and human resource adjustments that require expenditures of time and energy. During just the past six years, regulations for screening tests have changed three times. There is a need to (a) focus on ensuring a continuum of care, (b) integrate screening into routine care, and (c) further develop call and recall systems that have efficient feedback and back-referral mechanisms between PHC facilities and referral-level hospitals.

The government of Mongolia recognizes the importance of providing population-based screening to improve health outcomes and reduce mortality and is committed to this effort. Aiming at overly broad health goals—for example, increasing life expectancy, reducing gaps in life expectancy, or decreasing the incidence of cancer—that are associated with factors beyond early detection creates the risk of exhausting the capacity and resources of the health system. A more specific definition of goals and outcomes—for example, increasing the percentage of cases diagnosed at earlier stages, increasing survival rates, and lowering the costs per detected case—is recommended to support population-based screening and ensure the longevity and health of the Mongolian population.

Recommendations

The United Nations General Assembly has declared 2021–2030 as the Decade of Healthy Ageing. On December 14, 2019, Resolution 75/131 was adopted, calling on member states to support and implement the strategy and framework on healthy aging (UN General Assembly 2020). The Decade of Healthy Ageing framework recommends four main areas of action (figure 3.5) and supports a multisector approach to healthy aging. As such, it is highly recommended that Mongolia adopt a participatory, inclusive approach to develop a national policy document that adapts the United Nations Decade of Healthy Ageing framework to the needs of the Mongolian population.

FIGURE 3.5 Action Areas of the United Nations Framework "A Decade of Healthy Ageing"

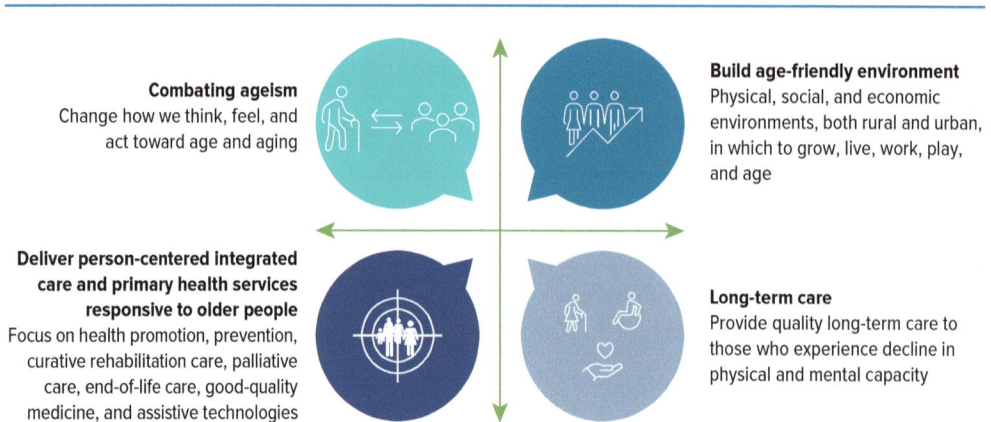

Combating ageism
Change how we think, feel, and act toward age and aging

Build age-friendly environment
Physical, social, and economic environments, both rural and urban, in which to grow, live, work, play, and age

Deliver person-centered integrated care and primary health services responsive to older people
Focus on health promotion, prevention, curative rehabilitation care, palliative care, end-of-life care, good-quality medicine, and assistive technologies

Long-term care
Provide quality long-term care to those who experience decline in physical and mental capacity

Source: Adapted from WHO 2021.

References

Asian Development Bank. 2020. *Country Diagnostic Study on Long-Term Care in Mongolia.* Metro Manila: Asian Development Bank. http://dx.doi.org/10.22617/TCS200320-2.

Center for Health Development. 2022. *Mongolia Health Indicators 2021.* Ulaanbaatar: Center for Health Development. https://ghdx.healthdata.org/record/mongolia-health-indicators-2021.

Government of Mongolia. 2011. "The Health Law of Mongolia 2011." Congress of Mongolia, Ulaanbaatar, May 5, 2011. https://legalinfo.mn/mn/detail/49.

Government of Mongolia. 2015. "The Law on Health Insurance: About Health Insurance; Updated Edition." Congress of Mongolia, Ulaanbaatar, January 29, 2015. https://legalinfo.mn/mn/detail/10922.

Government of Mongolia. 2017a. "MNS 5292: 2017: Structure and Activities of Family Health Centers." MongoliaLaws (database). https://www.mongolialaws.org/p-355045-mns-5292-2017.aspx.

Government of Mongolia. 2017b. "Resolution No. 197: Approval of Procedures, Additions, and Amendments to Appendices of Decisions, July 4, 2017." Government of Mongolia, Ulaanbaatar.

Health Insurance General Office. 2021. *Health Insurance Fund Indicators 2021.* https://emd.gov.mn/news/118.

Ministry of Health. 2017. "Health Minister Order A/129: Re-approving the List of Care and Services Provided at the Family Health Center, April 4, 2017." Ministry of Health, Ulaanbaatar.

Ministry of Health. 2018. "Health Minister Order No. A256: Procedures for Referring a Citizen from a Family, Soum, or Village Health Center to a Hospital for Medical Referral Care and Services, June 08, 2018." Ministry of Health, Ulaanbaatar.

Ministry of Health. 2020a. *Fourth National STEP Survey on the Prevalence of Non-Communicable Disease and Injury Risk Factors—2019.* Ulaanbaatar: Ministry of Health.

Ministry of Health. 2020b. "Health Minister Order No. A/179: About the Approval of Accreditation Criteria for Screening Primary Health Centers, 2020." Ministry of Health, Ulaanbaatar.

National Health Insurance Board. 2019. National Health Insurance Board Resolution No. 23 Amount of Payment from the Health Insurance Fund for Assistance and Services Provided by Home, Country, and Village Health Centers, November 18, 2019." National Health Insurance Board, Ulaanbaatar. https://legalinfo.mn/mn/detail?lawId=210264&showType=1.

National Health Insurance Board. 2022. "National Health Insurance Board Resolution No. 5 Re-approving the Payment Amount and Payment Procedure, March 23, 2022." National Health Insurance Board, Ulaanbaatar.

Secretariat of the State Great Hural. 2016. "Mongolia Sustainable Development Vision 2030." Secretariat of the State Great Hural, Ulaanbaatar. https://policy.asiapacificenergy.org/sites/default/files/Mongolia%20Sustainable%20Development%20Vision%202030%20%28EN%29.pdf.

UN (United Nations) General Assembly. 2020. "Resolution Adopted by the General Assembly on 14 December 2020 [without Reference to a Main Committee (A/75/L.47 and A/75/L.47/Add.1)] 75/131. United Nations Decade of Healthy Ageing (2021–2030)." A/Res/75/131, UN General Assembly, New York. https://documents.un.org/doc/undoc/gen/n20/363/87/pdf/n2036387.pdf?token=kRDmqstM0RRWfAKjk2&fe=true.

WHO (World Health Organization). 2013. "Mongolia Health System Review." Health Systems in Transition 3 (2), World Health Organization, Regional Office for the Western Pacific, Manila. https://apps.who.int/iris/handle/10665/207531.

WHO (World Health Organization). 2021. "Decade of Healthy Ageing: Baseline Report—Summary." World Health Organization, Geneva.

CHAPTER 4

United Arab Emirates: Leveraging a Crisis to Advance Integrated Older-Adult Care

Omniyat M. Al Hajeri, Sameh El-Saharty,
Hamed A. Al Hashemi, Sara Barada,
Arwa Al-Modwahi, and Anderson Stanciole

Key Messages

- In many countries, rising numbers of older adults pose challenges for the delivery of routine health services but also for the response to pandemics. To address this challenge and respond to the COVID-19 pandemic, Abu Dhabi deployed an innovative program—the Population-at-Risk Program—to limit COVID-19 infections among older adults and other vulnerable groups. This hybrid service delivery model combined telehealth consultations with home visits from providers, when required.

- The program effectively protected older adults from COVID-19, improved some indicators for chronic disease management, and yielded cost savings by reducing in-person clinic visits and hospitalizations.

- Population-at-Risk accelerated the uptake of digital health tools among vulnerable older adults. Following the acute phase of COVID-19, health authorities are expanding the program to cover larger segments of the population. Innovative care solutions to protect fragile older people in emergencies can yield wider health benefits for the population during noncrisis times.

Aging Populations and the COVID-19 Pandemic

Around 10 million people currently live in the United Arab Emirates, a number expected to reach around 11.1 million within seven years—by 2030 (Bardsley 2022). Although the population is mostly young, the number of people ages 65 and older—currently about 1 percent of the total (World Bank 2020)—has risen steadily over the past decade and is projected to reach 16 percent of the population by 2050 (DR Barometer 2023). This demographic transition will increase the burden of noncommunicable diseases (NCDs) and the demand for health services, which will put upward pressure on health expenditure.

The United Arab Emirates has achieved improvements in infant mortality and life expectancy, yet the rate of noncommunicable diseases remains high. Cardiovascular diseases, for example, are the leading cause of death in the country (IHME 2023). The prevalence of diabetes is among the highest in the world. More than 16 percent of the population, according to the International Diabetes Federation, have diabetes, and diabetes is the fifth-most common cause of death. In 2019, just three diseases—cardiovascular diseases, cancer, and respiratory diseases—accounted for approximately two-thirds (42 percent, 17 percent, and 5.8 percent, respectively) of all deaths in the country (Abu Dhabi Department of Health 2020).

In each of these three categories, the older-adult population has the highest percentage of deaths among the population of Abu Dhabi, the capital. The elderly are the most affected subgroup of all. In 2019, about 41 percent of persons who died of cardiovascular diseases and more than 73 percent of persons who died of respiratory diseases were 60 or older. In 2018, 42 percent of cancer-related deaths were among persons 65 and older.

From the outset of the COVID-19 pandemic, the United Arab Emirates' forward-thinking approach to health care served as a strong foundation to meet the challenges. Sound leadership, vision, effective policy making, and the use of financial resources and cross-sectoral collaboration led to the implementation of innovative programs that protected the population, including the most vulnerable. The country's COVID-19 response was aided by good health communications; robust testing, tracing, and monitoring; the widespread practice of physical distancing; and the provision of health services through a well-organized workforce and infrastructure.

Mitigating the Disruptions to Health Care Provision for Older Adults

The United Arab Emirates announced its first case of COVID-19 on January 29, 2020. The federal and emirate authorities promptly launched an early-response strategy that featured robust testing and contact tracing across the country. Lockdown measures were introduced rapidly. By September 2020, the emergency use of the Sinopharm vaccine had been authorized for frontline workers and others most at risk of infection.[1]

As in other countries, the surge of COVID-19-related hospitalizations sucked up health system resources, skewing and disrupting the entire spectrum of normal health care services, especially elective care and care for patients with chronic diseases. In response, Abu Dhabi's Department of Health and the Abu Dhabi Public Health Center took an immediate, proactive approach to meeting the needs of high-risk patients, particularly the elderly and individuals with a history of chronic conditions such as cardiovascular diseases, cancer, and diabetes.

Integrated Care through the Population-at-Risk Program

In March 2020, the Department of Health and the Abu Dhabi Public Health Center introduced the Abu Dhabi Population-at-Risk Program (Abu Dhabi Department of Health Circular 10/2020), aimed at reducing the risk of COVID-19 infections among the city's high-risk population by ensuring that patients were receiving essential care. The at-risk population was defined as patients of all ages with specific noncommunicable diseases, 90 percent of whom were covered by the *Thiqa*[2] insurance program for nationals and their dependents, about 44 percent of whom were elderly.

In light of the emergency, a hybrid model of service delivery was developed. Virtual visits on a telehealth platform were combined with "at-your-doorstep care" in the form of both routine and COVID-19-related testing, medications, and home visits. This model of integrated care delivery was supported by the Remote-Care Platform, which allowed providers to connect with enrolled patients online and provide them with services. At all visits, patients received information on how to manage their chronic conditions and referrals to appropriate care pathways. The program had four modules: data-driven analysis and insights, virtual care, a hybrid model of care, and a package of communications planning, health promotions, and guidelines supplied to care providers and patients through various channels.

The Population-at-Risk Program was rolled out in Abu Dhabi in March 2020 following a short pilot and was implemented in three phases (box 4.1). Phase 1 identified and enrolled patients. Phase 2 rolled out the program throughout the emirate. Phase 3 introduced remote-care monitoring. The patient's journey was planned in an integrated, holistic way across all three phases—from patient identification and registration to teleconsultations with a nurse or doctor, home visits, medication delivery, and remote-care monitoring (figure 4.1).

Phase 1: Identifying and Enrolling Patients (March–July 2020)

The program began in March 2020 by identifying eligible high-risk patients using claims data from Abu Dhabi's Knowledge Engine for Health. The Department of Health used a health risk matrix provided by the National Health

---

BOX 4.1 Five Objectives of the Population-at-Risk Program

1. Provide "at-your-doorstep" care to persons most vulnerable to COVID-19 through the delivery of COVID-19 testing, medications, and home visits in order to reduce infection contraction

2. Activate an integrated model of care for the elderly and for patients suffering from chronic diseases and provide education and awareness on how to manage these conditions

3. Ensure equitable access to health care for the chronically ill if they prefer not to visit a facility physically during the pandemic

4. Provide comprehensive medical home care in a hybrid fashion (home visits along with virtual visits via the telehealth platform)

5. Enable evidence-based, data-driven interventions to identify and prioritize community needs

FIGURE 4.1 Population-at-Risk Program in the United Arab Emirates: The Journey of a Patient

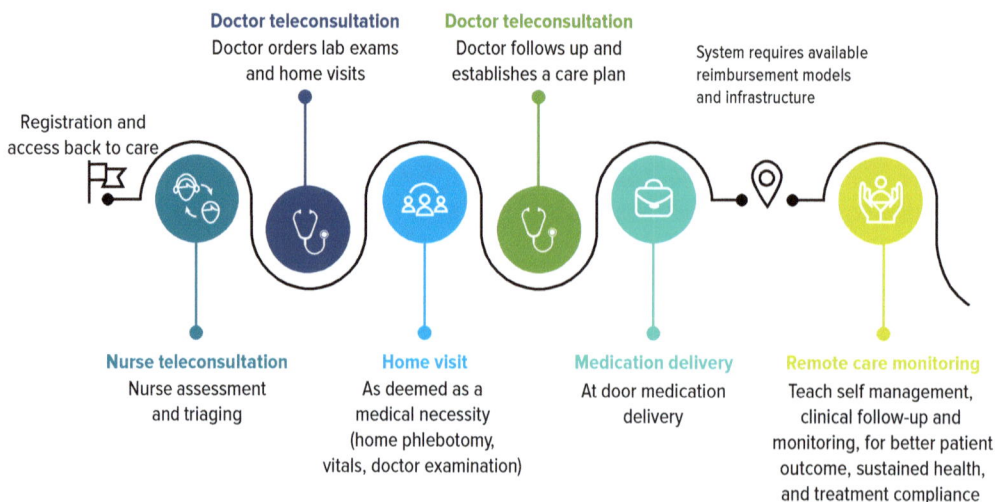

Source: Abu Dhabi Department of Health.

Insurance Company (Daman) to identify eligible patients. Approximately 0.28 percent of the population was classified as high-risk. Table 4.1 shows their distribution by sex, type of insurance, and age.

The Abu Dhabi Public Health Center selected 2,000 high-risk patients to test out the telehealth services. Each was assigned to a facility to which they had previously made recurring visits and was briefed on the program's benefits and enrollment process. Of the initial pilot cohort, three-quarters (1,500) ultimately enrolled.

In August 2020 outcomes of the pilot phase were assessed using data on enrollment, patient activity, services rendered, and patient and provider feedback. It was observed that some patients found it hard to use the telehealth services because of their age, medical condition, or lack of digital literacy. To increase participation, the review team added the option of contacting patients by phone or, if needed, through home visits, and the program transitioned to a hybrid model (home visits and telehealth).

The program was then expanded to cover the most vulnerable patients with chronic diseases in Abu Dhabi, including patients younger than 60. Out of 33,141 patients contacted, more than half (21,804) were successfully enrolled. The list of eligible noncommunicable diseases was expanded to include hypertension, renal disease, and immune diseases. Figure 4.2 shows the number of patients who chose to enroll out of the total number identified as eligible.

Phase 2: Implementation (July–November 2020 and beyond)

Following the pilot, six licensed health care providers were selected (through a request for proposals) to offer the following services:

1. Have a licensed clinician contact and assess the health status of patients via telemedicine

TABLE 4.1 Distribution of High-Risk Patients in Abu Dhabi, by Sex, Insurance, and Age Group, 2019

Indicator	Distribution (%)
Sex	
Male	54.24
Female	45.76
Type of insurance	
Thiqa	40.61
Basic	31.77
Enhanced	27.59
Others	0.04
Age group (years)	
Under 60	56.26
60+	43.74

Source: Based on Abu Dhabi Department of Health data.

FIGURE 4.2 Numbers and Percentages of Patients Enrolled in the Population-at-Risk Program in the United Arab Emirates

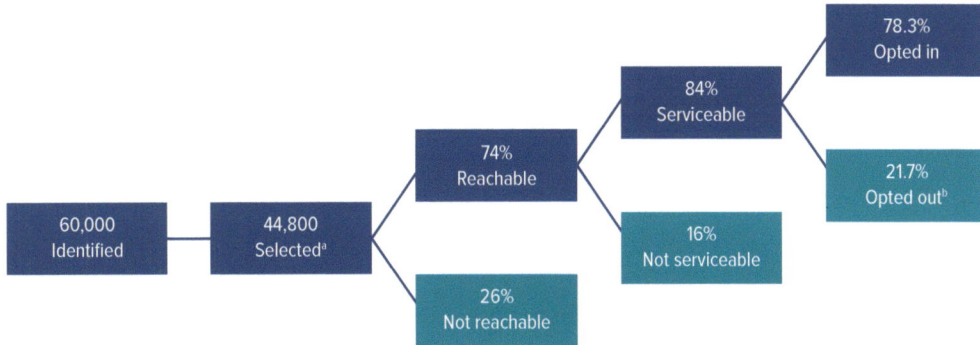

Source: Abu Dhabi Department of Health data.
a. The remainder of patients (15,200) were excluded because they were enrolled in other programs.
b. Patients who opted out of the program still received a call from a nurse to ensure that their care was not disrupted.

2. Give advice, write prescriptions, refill medications through teleprescription, and issue referrals to specialists

3. Deliver medication to the patient's doorstep

4. Provide "at-home" specialized interventions and visits to mobile clinics specifically for polymerase chain reaction testing for COVID-19

5. Educate patients by supporting disease-specific health promotion campaigns

6. Administer COVID-19 and flu vaccines

7. Follow up as required through telehealth consultations or home visits.

The Department of Health and the Abu Dhabi Public Health Center provided participating health care providers with a list of their allocated patients' names, contact numbers, addresses, and the chronic diseases to be targeted. They also gave providers access to interactive maps, burden of disease data and numbers to be served, specialized educational tips about each chronic disease and about COVID-19, and recorded messages to inform patients who could not read.

Through the Remote-Care Platform, providers conducted telehealth services and completed medical recordkeeping (box 4.2 provides more information on the platform's features). Providers were also allowed to conduct consultations over the phone to reach patients who were not comfortable with the digital telehealth platform. Through the Malaffi provider portal, providers were also able to access patients' medical histories, regardless of where they had previously been treated.

Phase 3: Remote-Care Monitoring (December 2020–June 2021)

Phase 3 started in December 2020, with the objective of enabling patients to self-manage their conditions, supported by clinical follow-up care and monitoring through the Remote-Care Platform. This third phase aimed to improve patient outcomes, increase treatment compliance, and sustain improvements in patient health. Success depended on the availability of suitable reimbursement models and infrastructure to move enrolled patients from the identification and activation phases into the third phase.

BOX 4.2 The Remote-Care Platform App

Developed in record time—four weeks—to support the Population-at-Risk Program, the Remote-Care Platform enabled patients to receive health services in their homes. Launched in March 2020, the phone-based app offered the following:

- The ability to book appointments or consultations with doctors via voice, video call, or texts.
- E-prescriptions and the delivery of medications to the patient's home.
- Online referrals by doctors for health care services and prescriptions.

  Within three months of launch (between April and June 2020),

- The Department of Health conducted 71 virtual trainings for the staff of all participating providers.
- Patients and general practitioners downloaded more than 35,000 applications.
- More than 22,648 patients were registered on the app.
- 2,762 physicians were registered on the app (70 percent were registered within two weeks of launch).
- 832 physicians were active on the platform (32 percent of total registered physicians).
- 98 operational medical providers were registered (18 facilities every week since the launch).

  Patients were assigned to the six participating public and private providers based on an established patient history at the facility. This strategy of matching patients with a familiar health care provider was intended to increase uptake.

Components of the Population-at-Risk Program

Communication and Marketing Plan

A key step in implementing the Population-at-Risk Program was to develop and roll out a communication and marketing campaign to support implementation. The program had three components:

- *Health promotion guidelines.* Health care providers were supplied with standardized information to help them provide better care to patients with specific chronic diseases during the COVID-19 pandemic. Guidelines and health messages tailored to the specific diseases covered in the program were circulated to all participating health care facilities.

- *Social media campaign.* Awareness messages were sent out via social media channels, and press releases were published in all traditional news media. An informational video was produced and circulated to the media to announce the program's launch, explain its goals, and provide the Abu Dhabi Public Health Center's WhatsApp number for inquiries.

- *Support email.* A dedicated email address was created for patients and providers to report any technical or other issues they experienced while downloading or using the Remote-Care app.

Program Governance

The Department of Health and the Abu Dhabi Public Health Center both participated in the executive leadership and management of the program. The Department of Health led planning, implementation, and risk management. An executive taskforce that included subject-matter experts advised the program team on key areas such as quality, primary care, finance, innovation, corporate communications, and public health. A multidisciplinary functional team coordinated with the participating public and private health providers.

The national health insurance company, Daman, was responsible for developing new reimbursement models for the program's virtual and home-care services. Figure 4.3 describes the program's governance and organizational structure and the role played by each level of management.

Program Outputs

As of June 2021, the program had reached more than 33,000 patients (74 percent of the identified at-risk population) and enrolled 66 percent of the patients who were able to be reached. More than 49,000 services were rendered, including virtual nurse assessments, teleconsultations, home visits, and medication deliveries (figure 4.4).

Table 4.2 presents a sample of the type and number of services provided by two of the participating private providers. The table highlights the wide variation in services between the two providers, mainly due to the difference in the number of enrollees in each facility.

FIGURE 4.3 Organizational Structure of the Population-at-Risk Program in the United Arab Emirates

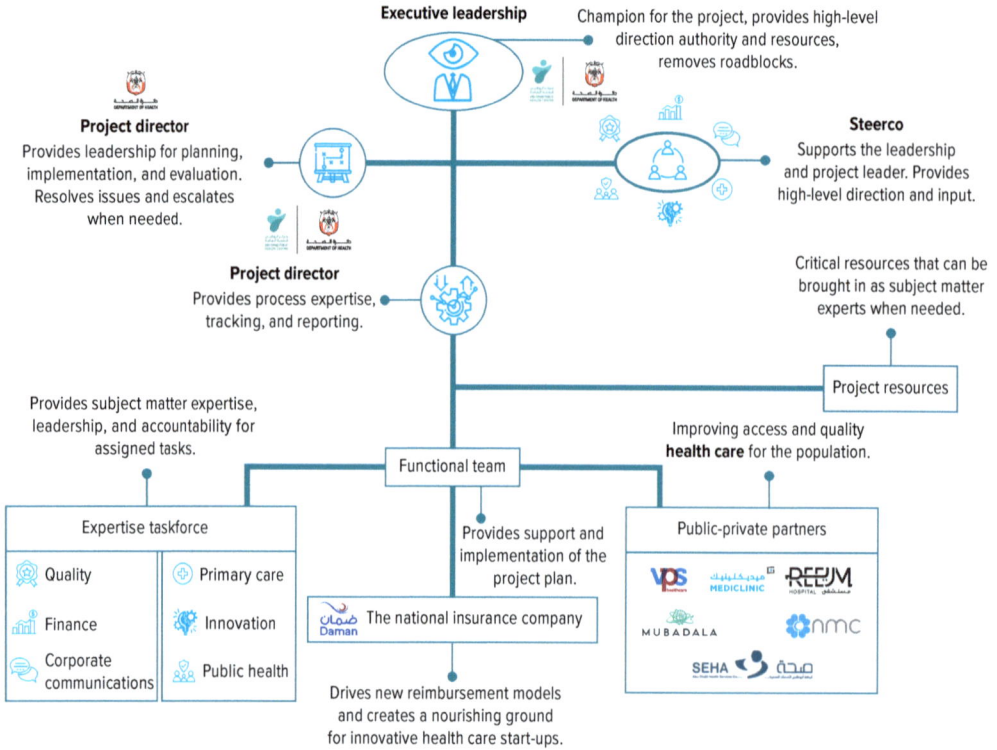

Executive leadership
Champion for the project, provides high-level direction authority and resources, removes roadblocks.

Project director
Provides leadership for planning, implementation, and evaluation. Resolves issues and escalates when needed.

Steerco
Supports the leadership and project leader. Provides high-level direction and input.

Project director
Provides process expertise, tracking, and reporting.

Critical resources that can be brought in as subject matter experts when needed.

Project resources

Provides subject matter expertise, leadership, and accountability for assigned tasks.

Improving access and quality **health care** for the population.

Functional team

Expertise taskforce
- Quality
- Finance
- Corporate communications
- Primary care
- Innovation
- Public health

Provides support and implementation of the project plan.

The national insurance company

Public-private partners

VPS
MEDICLINIC
REEM HOSPITAL
MUBADALA
nmc
SEHA

Drives new reimbursement models and creates a nourishing ground for innovative health care start-ups.

Source: Abu Dhabi Department of Health 2020.

FIGURE 4.4 Services Rendered by the Population-at-Risk Program in the United Arab Emirates

Nurse assessments	36,534
Doctor teleconsultations	4,673
Home visits	1,837
Medication delivery	2,947

41,207 — Phone calls undertaken

10,691 — Hours spent on clinical calls

Source: Based on Abu Dhabi Department of Health data.

TABLE 4.2 Services Delivered by Two Private Providers under the Population-at-Risk Program in the United Arab Emirates

Services	Private provider 1	Private provider 2
Physician teleconsultations	301	6,213
Nurse teleconsultations	1,230	2,886
Nurse home visits	350	2,037
Prescriptions	—	3,883
Medication dispensed	—	5,923
Medication delivered	34	—
Flu vaccinations	—	63
COVID-19 vaccinations	—	319
Referrals	3	127

Source: Based on Abu Dhabi Department of Health data.
Note: — = not available.

Lessons Learned

Through its Population-at-Risk Program, Abu Dhabi turned the COVID-19 pandemic into an opportunity to accelerate the introduction and widespread adoption of digital health tools and to involve both public and private providers in a proactive, innovative program designed to protect the health of at-risk populations.

Benefits

Management's Perspective

Program managers identified several program benefits in the areas of safety, access, patient experience, cost, and patient outcomes:

- A reduction in the risk of COVID-19 infection and better management of chronic disease conditions
- Expanded access to care for the high-risk population through telehealth and the Remote-Care app
- Implementation of specific interventions targeted exclusively to the high-risk population
- Improved patient experience that reduced the burden of care for the at-risk population and enhanced coordination and integration of care
- Improved outcomes for diabetic patients; of 593 patients who provided their glycated hemoglobin A1c results both before and after enrolling with one of four private providers, more than 45 percent showed improvement in their diabetes management

- Proactive identification of patients who required urgent or higher levels of care
- Cost savings as a result of preventing more than 10,000 unnecessary hospital or clinic visits and admissions (box 4.3).

Providers' Perspective

Three of the participating private providers provided feedback on the benefits of the program, summarized in the following four areas:

- Greater access to care through the Remote-Care Platform and home visits and improved patient safety through remote care
- Improved patient engagement and satisfaction due to the convenience of accessing care from their home through telehealth and home care services and reengagement with a health care provider
- Lower costs due to the efficient use of clinical resources—which cut staffing and overhead costs and lowered the number of hospital visits and admissions—and to earlier detection of clinical complications
- Enhanced patient outcomes and disease management for high-risk patient populations.

Patients' Perspective

The Abu Dhabi Department of Health commissioned two surveys in 2021 to gather feedback on the performance of the program and patient satisfaction. A sample of 6,858 patients were surveyed across all participating providers. The two surveys yielded consistent scores of 86.1 out of 100 and 85.2 out of 100, respectively, for the program's overall performance (figure 4.5).

Table 4.3 summarizes four patient case studies created by one of the participating private providers. The study highlights the benefits and the outcomes of the program interventions.

BOX 4.3 Estimated Cost Savings: Telemedicine Outpatient Consultations versus Face-to-Face Visits

One private provider estimated that using telemedicine services instead of face-to-face consultation in the first quarter of 2022 alone resulted in efficiency and cost savings of Dh 237,000 (dirhams) for its patient cohort.

During the same three-month period, revenue rose by 7.5 percent. In addition, 52 percent of the provider's total revenue was generated by new patients accessing the telemedicine services, indicating that the program clearly generated new demand for the provider's services.

FIGURE 4.5 Results of Two Patient Surveys of Satisfaction with the Population-at-Risk Program in the United Arab Emirates, 2021

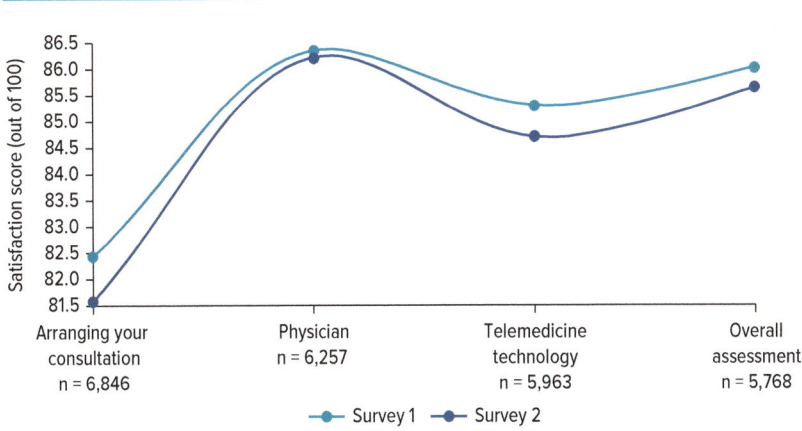

Source: Abu Dhabi Department of Health patient surveys.
Note: Findings based on two surveys that the Abu Dhabi Department of Health commissioned in 2021. The sample size is 6,858.

TABLE 4.3 Patient Case Studies and Outcomes Resulting from Enrollment in the Population-at-Risk Program

Patient case study	Program intervention	Outcome
Female 64 years old with known type 2 diabetes, hypertension, hyperlipidemia, and chronic kidney disease, which the daughter described as mild to moderate. Patient had not seen a nephrologist.	Upon investigation, the physician found that the patient had advanced renal failure level 4, almost level 5. Urgent nephrologist referral was made.	Patient reengaged with medical services and now has a multidisciplinary team and treatment plan, which is reviewed regularly.
Female 74 years old with type 2 diabetes, hypertension, and heart disease. Patient takes long-term aspirin and another antithrombotic agent.	After physician teleconsultation, the doctor ordered a nurse home visit for blood collection. Blood tests revealed that the patient was severely anemic, with a very low hemoglobin of 5.5.	Doctor arranged urgent admission for the patient. Blood transfusion was given, and the underlying cause of severe anemia was investigated and treated.
Female renal transplant patient. Follow-up was coordinated with Cleveland Clinic, where the transplant was performed. Patient was out of touch with services due to the COVID-19 pandemic.	After physician teleconsultation, the doctor ordered a nurse home visit for blood collection. Her tacrolimus dose level was subsequently adjusted.	Patient reengaged with medical services and is now on an optimized treatment regimen.
Male with high-risk chronic disease comorbidities.	After physician teleconsultation, the doctor ordered a nurse home visit for administration of the pneumovax vaccine.	Patient received an immunization without having to make an in-person facility visit, thus reducing the likelihood of exposure to COVID-19.

Source: Data from private providers.

Challenges

Despite the program's success, the program leadership identified several challenges:

- A high percentage of elderly patients had difficulty using the digital technology.
- Some patients were reluctant to enroll because of a lack of trust in the effectiveness of the program.
- Some patients simply preferred one-on-one physical interaction to virtual care.
- Only a limited number of providers registered with the program.
- The infrastructure to support remote care was insufficient.
- There was a lack of standardized processes for enrolling patients and monitoring success.

   Three participating private providers outlined the following challenges:

- *Lack of understanding of program benefits.* Many patients lacked understanding and awareness of the program's benefits because telemedicine had not been widely used in the United Arab Emirates. Cultural barriers may have contributed to low patient enrollment. Patients were more likely to wait and seek care when they were symptomatic or their health was deteriorating.
- *Low patient digital literacy.* Many of the patients, especially those ages 60 and older, were unfamiliar with using an app for telemedicine consultations. Others did not have a smartphone, tablet, or computer capable of signing on and accessing digital features such as teleconferencing.
- *Lack of provider resources.* One provider found it difficult to put together a team of licensed health care professionals to follow up with enrolled patients. This difficulty was exacerbated by staff shortages during the pandemic caused by burnout and high rates of COVID-19 infection among staff.
- *Service continuity.* The lack of a face-to-face initial meeting between patients and physicians may have hampered the development of a trustful relationship. Indeed, as the number of COVID-19 cases started to fall, some patients switched to visiting their doctor for face-to-face consultations. As a result, the number of patients participating in the program declined significantly.
- *Reimbursement model.* One provider, a private hospital, said that the reimbursement model was not well developed and did not make the program financially viable for the hospital.

Next Steps

The Department of Health extended the duration of the Population-at-Risk Program several times, the last being a three-month extension issued in December 2021. Nevertheless, some services such as medication delivery are still being provided.

   Of the six providers that participated in the program,

- Two exited the program but continued to provide telehealth services to their patients using their own telehealth platforms.

- Four continued to collaborate with the Department of Health and the Abu Dhabi Public Health Center program team and provide data on their patient cohort, including outcome data.
- One provider is expanding the program to integrate wearables into the process to track additional clinical indicators such as blood pressure, glucose levels, and body mass index.

On the regulator side, the Abu Dhabi Public Health Center is planning to extend the Remote-Care Platform to provide telehealth services to a new cohort of patients: people of determination (that is, people with disabilities). The Abu Dhabi Public Health Center has partnered with the Zayed Higher Organization for People of Determination to design and implement the new program, which is expected to launch in 2023.

The Department of Health is working with its technology partner to develop an updated, enhanced version of the Remote-Care Platform. Using the updated platform, the Department of Health plans to expand coverage to all primary care patients as part of its virtual care initiatives. The redesigned platform will now include recurring subscription fees.

Implications for Other Contexts

Providing virtual care to and remotely monitoring high-risk patients require financial investments in infrastructure and human resources, which may be a challenge for low- or even middle-income countries. Nonetheless, the Abu Dhabi Population-at-Risk Program offers lessons that other countries can use to enhance access, reduce costs, and improve outcomes for the elderly and other high-risk patient groups. Seven lessons stand out:

- *Population targeting using tools and data.* The use of existing data, along with analytical tools, can help to identify high-risk patients more accurately. Accurate identification is the first step in rolling out a targeted intervention.

- *Piloting and scaling.* It can be helpful to pilot such programs on a small initial population of patients and then adjust and scale up the program in accordance with the measured evidence.

- *The role of patient engagement.* Patient awareness, mobilization, engagement, and education are critical for the success and sustainability of such programs.

- *Measurement and evaluation.* Defining success at the very outset in the form of structural, process, and outcome measures is necessary in order to assess program performance and determine whether midcourse adjustments are needed.

- *Collaboration in service delivery.* Promoting public and private partnerships among regulators, providers, software developers, and payers creates the collaboration needed to deliver an integrated, targeted model of care.

- *Innovation in service delivery.* Providing a hybrid mix of virtual care via telehealth and mobile apps (where possible), combined with in-home primary care, can broaden access and lead to greater patient satisfaction, better outcomes, and cost savings.

- *Financing.* Introducing flexible, innovative reimbursement models is key to enhancing access to, and the affordability of, such programs and to incentivizing both providers and patients to participate.

As the adoption of digital health delivery models gains ground and becomes more widespread, additional evidence can be gathered on the benefits of leveraging technology to improve access to care and, ultimately, improve outcomes for the elderly and other high-risk patient populations.

Meanwhile, two overarching insights emerge. First, a comprehensive approach to the design and implementation of technology-enabled interventions is recommended. Second, the collaboration of policy makers, providers, payers, patients, and technology service providers is a critical component in the design of solutions that will improve the health of high-risk patients.

Notes

1. Refer to "Vaccines against COVID-19 in the UAE," https://u.ae/en/information-and-services/justice-safety-and-the-law/handling-the-Covid-19-outbreak/vaccines-against-Covid-19-in-the-uae.
2. *Thiqa* means trust or confidence in Arabic.

References

Abu Dhabi Department of Health. 2020. *Death Statistics 2019*. Abu Dhabi: Department of Health. https://scad.gov.ae/documents/20122/2310804/Death%2520Statistics_2019_Annual_Yearly_en.pdf.

Bardsley, Daniel. 2022. "Dubai Population to Surge to Nearly 6m in 20 Years amid Urban Transformation." *The National (UAE)*, August 2, 2022. https://www.thenationalnews.com/uae/2022/01/23/dubai-population-to-surge-to-nearly-6m-in-20-years-amid-urban-transformation/#:~:text=What%20the%20future%20holds%20UN,and%2014.8m%20in%202100.

DR Barometer. 2023. *The DR Barometer Study: United Arab Emirates Overview*. Toronto: DR Barometer. https://drbarometer.com/evidence/explore-the-data/united-arab-emirates.

IHME (Institute for Health Metrics and Evaluation). 2023. "United Arab Emirates: Top 10 Causes of Total Number of Deaths in 2019 and Percent Change 2009–2019, All Ages Combined." IHME, University of Washington School of Medicine, Seattle. https://www.healthdata.org/united-arab-emirates.

World Bank. 2020. World Development Indicators (database). World Bank, Washington, DC. https://data.worldbank.org/indicator/SP.POP.65UP.TO.ZS?locations=AE&name_desc=false.

CHAPTER 5

Long-Term Care for Aging Populations in Africa: Current Landscape, Key Challenges, and Policy Considerations

Zhanlian Feng, Natalie Mulmule, Xiaohui Hou, and
Jigyasa Sharma

Key Messages

- Sub-Saharan Africa's population is still young, on average, but the absolute number of Africans age 60 or older is surging, placing traditional family-based care models under strain. Formal long-term care (LTC) systems for older people are nascent across the continent.

- In Africa as elsewhere, most countries aim for balanced, mixed LTC systems combining informal and formal services. Mixed systems may best reconcile traditional norms, current labor market shifts (for example, women's paid employment), and individual preferences.

- To promote sustainability, most countries direct LTC investment toward home- and community-based care solutions. Countries can support family caregivers with training, counseling, respite care, and other measures.

- Some countries choose to "mainstream" support for older adults by integrating healthy-aging policies into broader socioeconomic development plans that benefit the whole population. The African Union (AU) Plan of Action on Ageing recommends this approach.

- Countries can leverage existing primary health care delivery to expand key facets of long-term care incrementally for older adults—for example, screening for noncommunicable diseases (NCDs) and help with medication management.

Africa's Looming Demographic Shift

With a median age of 19 years, Africa's population is considerably younger than that of other regions in the world (UN DESA 2022). At the same time, Africa's older population is not only living longer but is expected to increase (He, Aboderin, and Adjaye-Gbewonyo 2020). According to projections, the percentage of Africa's population age 60 and older will rise from 5.5 percent in 2022 to 8.7 percent by 2050 (UN DESA 2022).

Although the percentage of adults 60 years and older is still small in comparison with other world regions, the absolute number of older people in Africa is large and will grow rapidly in the coming decades (table 5.1). In 2022, about 78.0 million people in Africa were 60 years of age or older (UN DESA 2022). This number is projected to reach 215.1 million by 2050, nearly tripling in less than 30 years. By this date, the over-60 population in Africa will outnumber the over-60 population in North America (125.6 million) and Latin America and the Caribbean (188.1 million) and will approach the size of Europe's over-60 population (252.1 million). Indeed, between now and 2050, the older population will increase faster in Africa (175.7 percent) than in any other region.

This increase in the number of older people between 2022 and 2050 is expected to proceed at a similar rate across all African subregions (figure 5.1) as well as countries (figure 5.2). Figure 5.2 presents the most populous country in each subregion: Ethiopia (East Africa), the Democratic Republic of Congo (Central Africa), the Arab Republic of Egypt (North Africa), South Africa (Southern Africa), and Nigeria (West Africa).

The unmet health care needs of Africa's older population are significantly higher than those of similar populations in higher-income settings (Aboderin 2019). The frailty of this population and the rates of disability are expected to rise due to the growing burden of noncommunicable diseases such as cardiovascular disease, musculoskeletal conditions, diabetes, and cancers (He, Aboderin, and Adjaye-Gbewonyo 2020). For example, in Ghana, 50 percent of people age 65–75

TABLE 5.1 Total Population and Population Age 60 and Older, by World Region, 2022 and 2050 (Projected)

Region	Total population (millions)		Population ages 60 and over				
			2022		2050		Percentage change in number, 2022–50
	2022	2050	Number (millions)	%	Number (millions)	%	
Africa	**1,426.7**	**2,485.1**	**78.0**	**5.5**	**215.1**	**8.7**	**175.7**
Asia	4,722.6	5,292.9	649.0	13.7	1,337.6	25.3	106.1
Europe	743.6	703.0	195.7	26.3	252.1	35.9	28.8
Latin America and the Caribbean	660.3	749.2	88.6	13.4	188.1	25.1	112.3
Northern America	376.9	421.4	89.3	23.7	125.6	29.8	40.7
Oceania	45.0	57.8	8.0	17.7	13.9	24.1	75.0

Source: UN DESA 2022.

FIGURE 5.1 Population Age 60 and Older in Africa and Its Subregions, 2022 and 2050 (Projected)

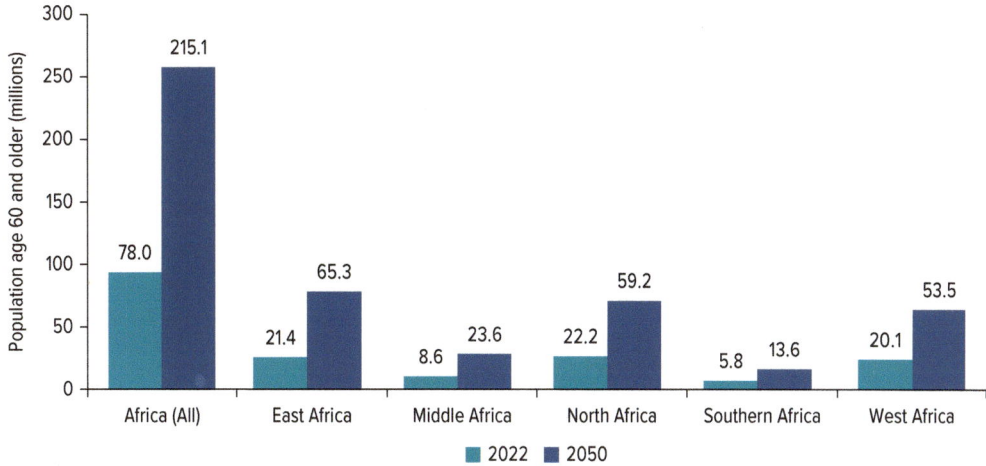

Source: UN DESA 2022.

FIGURE 5.2 Population Age 60 and Older in Select African Countries, 2022 and 2050 (Projected)

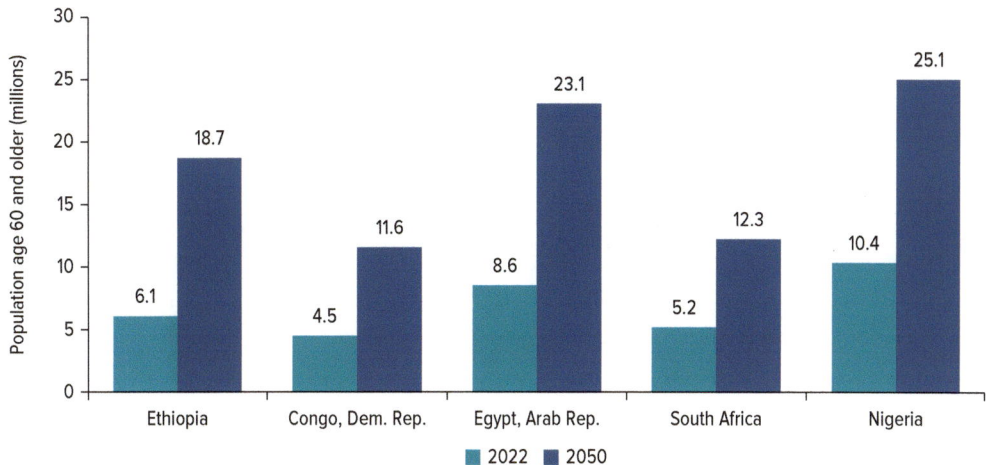

Source: UN DESA 2022.

require some assistance with activities of daily living (ADLs). In South Africa, about 35 percent of persons age 65 or older and 45 percent of persons age 75 or older require assistance with ADLs (WHO 2017).

The steady increase in the size of older populations, coupled with the rising burden of noncommunicable diseases across Africa, calls for efforts to strengthen the health care system and develop organized LTC services across the continent.

Cardiovascular disease is the leading cause of death among older Africans, with ischemic heart disease responsible for 15.7 percent of deaths in both men and women over 60 (He, Aboderin, and Adjaye-Gbewonyo 2020). Although rates of cardiovascular disease are currently lower in Africa than in other parts of the world, the low levels of awareness, preventive screening, and treatment mean that these conditions often go undetected. The lack of access to primary care is another reason why many noncommunicable diseases, such as cardiovascular disease, go undetected.

Prostate cancer is another major contributor to deaths among older men in Africa (He, Aboderin, and Adjaye-Gbewonyo 2020). In 2018, only 7 percent of Kenyan men age 50–54 had ever been screened for prostate cancer (He, Aboderin, and Adjaye-Gbewonyo 2020). Historically, many older Africans have been able to rely on family members for care, but multiple issues—ranging from demographic shifts and rapid sociocultural change to economic stress, rural-to-urban migration, human immunodeficiency virus/acquired immunodeficiency syndrome (HIV/AIDS), and other acute crises—pose significant challenges for this model of family-based elder care (Aboderin and Ferreira 2008).

The Current Landscape of Long-Term Care

Family Caregivers, the Backbone of Long-Term Care, Are under Increasing Strain

In Sub-Saharan Africa, the family unit is the primary provider of LTC services for older family members. This ingrained cultural practice diminishes the general population's desire for policy interventions to institute organized care for the elderly (Aboderin 2019; Lloyd-Sherlock 2014; WHO 2017). Additionally, due to fiscal concerns, many Sub-Saharan African governments see an expansion of formal LTC services as unaffordable and not a priority, given that families continue to consider themselves responsible for the care of their elderly (Aboderin 2019; Scheil-Adlung 2015).

Even though family caregiving has been the norm in Africa, it is not always the best option for older adults needing complex care. The quality of caregiving naturally varies from family to family, and most relatives lack formal caregiving skills. For example, there is a significant knowledge gap around how to care for people with dementia in many Sub-Saharan African countries. This lack of understanding can lead to abandonment, neglect, abuse, and, in extreme cases, death. Older women are disproportionately affected by unhelpful cultural attitudes. For example, in Tanzania in 2013, about 765 older adults were killed on suspicion that they were witches; 505 of them (two-thirds) were women (Mussie et al. 2022). Poverty and vulnerable employment opportunities also affect the quality of care that families provide to their older relatives. Many families cannot afford to care for an older relative and pursue an economic opportunity at the same time. The financial strain of caregiving can also adversely affect the caregiver's physical and mental health, particularly in households with dependent children (WHO 2017).

As a result, the traditional system of family support has been showing signs of weakening. Many factors underlie this structural breakdown, especially rural-to-urban migration and increased female participation in the labor force (WHO 2017).

Traditionally, women—daughters, daughters-in-law, and wives—have provided most of the caregiving (Aboderin 2019; WHO 2017). The recent surge in female workforce participation has clear implications for home-based elder care. Rural-to-urban migration is also weakening the traditional structure of family support. Many young people are choosing to move to urban areas in pursuit of economic opportunities, resulting in the isolation of older family members left behind in rural areas (Aboderin and Ferreira 2008; WHO 2017). This cultural shift is creating a significant need for formal LTC services.

The HIV/AIDS epidemic has also strained the traditional family structure. Despite some encouraging trends in HIV/AIDS cases, the epidemic has had a devastaing impact on the Sub-Saharan African population (Aboderin and Ferreira 2008). The effects of the epidemic place older adults in a precarious position. HIV/AIDS mortality rates among the younger generation raise concerns that the elderly will not have the traditional support of their children or younger family members (Aboderin 2019; WHO 2017). Older adults may have to care for their adult children, sick family members, or grandchildren orphaned or left behind by migrant parents (He, Aboderin, and Adjaye-Gbewonyo 2020; Scheil-Adlung 2015). Older adults must also balance their own increasingly complex health needs with such caregiving responsibilities.

Formal LTC Services Are Scant, Urban-Centric, and Hindered by Financing and Workforce Shortages

Currently, formal LTC services are very limited or nonexistent in most parts of Africa. Exisiting or emerging LTC services are concentrated in two extremes—charitable services for the most destitute and private for-profit services for persons able to afford them (Aboderin 2019). Most forms of organized care are available predominantly in urban areas, further isolating people living in rural areas (WHO 2017).

Organized home-based care appears to be gaining popularity in some African countries since it supports older adults who desire to remain at home. For example, in Ghana's private health care sector, home-based LTC services are available to persons who can afford them (Scheil-Adlung 2015). South Africa is one of the few Sub-Saharan African countries that has residential facilities for the elderly. However, the eligibility criteria for facility-based services are very strict, and applicants must go through rigorous means testing. Admission is dependent on the availability of beds, many facilities are located in urban centers, and services in rural areas often lack basic health care equipment or medicines (Mussie et al. 2022).

Financing appears to be a key issue hampering the expansion of LTC services across the continent. Programs and facilities are financed from a variety of sources—donors, nongovernmental organizations, religious organizations, and out-of-pocket payments. Even in South Africa, where 74 percent of facilities receive government subsidies, donations and out-of-pocket payments are needed to cover the costs of care (Scheil-Adlung 2015). The few facilities that do exist tend to be poorly maintained. They can be unhygienic and cramped and lack reliable access to electricity or water (WHO 2017). Funding challenges can also affect the provision of medications for conditions such as arthritis, hypertension, and diabetes, which are common in the LTC population (Mussie et al. 2022).

Historical and cultural barriers also affect the expansion of LTC services in Africa. Institutional care in Africa has roots in colonialism and is perceived as a "Western solution" to elder care. Many nursing homes or residential care facilities were originally established by colonists and then eventually opened up to the native African population. The legacy of colonization and segmentation of the population using residential care facilities may discourage native African people from considering institutional care as a desirable or viable option. In South Africa, most residential care homes are patronized by the white population (Scheil-Adlung 2015).

There is a dearth of qualified health care professionals and a severe shortage of LTC health workers in African countries (WHO 2017). Dementia care specialists are rare, and the overall level of expertise in geriatric care among health care professionals is low (WHO 2017). The lack of an adequate, well-trained, and stable workforce presents a significant challenge to improving access to and quality of LTC services. In addition, health care education needs to be standardized to ensure that health care workers have the appropriate knowledge, including training in geriatric care, to provide older people with good-quality LTC care.

A Few Integrated Care Delivery Models for Older Adults Exist, but Sustainability Is a Concern

Various LTC delivery models or programs were identified from publicly available sources, all with limited integration of care and services (table 5.2). These models or programs nonetheless provide examples of ways to address the multifaceted issues and care needs of older people in various country contexts. Most of these models focus on expanding access to home-based care. But a few, including Rand Aid, in South Africa, and Sierra Leone Society for the Welfare of the Aged, in Sierra Leone, are centered around providing institutional care. These programs are financed mostly through donations and grants, apart from Care for the Aged, in Zambia, which is financed through the Ministry of Community Development and Social Services.

The insitutional care models tend to employ more health care professionals, whereas many of the home-based care models are staffed by volunteers, with few clinical staff. It is difficult to sustain, educate, and supervise a volunteer workforce (WHO 2017). Financially, these programs rely primarily on donations or out-of-pocket payments, with a few funded by the government. Such models are best suited to geographic areas where out-of-pocket health care payments are more feasible or where strong ties with donor partners exist, but they do not solve the challenge of expanding into rural areas where the need is great and resources are scarce.

Policy Framework on Aging

Two international frameworks drive policy development on aging in Africa—the Madrid International Plan of Action on Ageing (MIPAA) and the AU Policy Framework and Plan of Action on Ageing. The MIPAA, which the United Nations established in 2002, aims to respond to the "opportunities and challenges of population ageing in the twenty-first century and to promote the

TABLE 5.2 Models of Integrated Care Delivery for Older Adults in Africa

Program or organization	Country	Number of persons covered	Key features
Ageing with a Smile Initiative	Gambia, The	—	• Is a community-based organization that promotes and protects the health of older people • Provides home-based care through a team of doctors, public health professionals, nurses, and social workers on a volunteer basis
Care 4 Aged Outreach	Ghana	—	• Creates individualized care plans with older adults and their families • Provides home-based services such as personal care, medical care, and house work • Is staffed largely by volunteers, many of them young people in the community
Care for the Aged	Zambia	—	• Is run by the Ministry of Community Development and Social Services, which runs two care homes and supports several others across Zambia through grants • Provides institutional and noninstitutional health care services • Has developed minimum standards of care for establishing and managing homes for older persons
HelpAge International	Congo, Dem. Rep.; Ethiopia; Ghana; Kenya; Mozambique; Tanzania; Uganda	—	• Seeks to secure reliable incomes for older people in several countries and improve health and care services by supporting health care facilities, working with local governments to advocate for older adults, and helping refugee communities
Rand Aid	South Africa	1,800–2,000	• Provides parallel long-term care institutional services to persons who can afford them and uses the profit generated to run facilities in areas of need
Sierra Leone Society for the Welfare of the Aged	Sierra Leone	—	• Provides shelter, care, and support to older people out of the King George VI Memorial Home, an elder home

Sources: For Ageing with a Smile Initiative, http://asigambia.weebly.com. For Care 4 Aged Outreach, https://care4aged.org. For Care for the Aged, https://www.mcdss.gov.zm/?page_id=2229. For HelpAge International, https://www.helpage.org/where-we-work/helpage-global-network-members-in-africa. For Rand Aid, https://randaid.co.za. For Sierra Leone Society for the Welfare of the Aged, Schneider 2020.
Note: — = not available.

development of a society for all ages" (United Nations 2002). It focuses on three priority areas: supporting the development of older persons, advancing health and well-being into old age, and ensuring enabling and supportive environments (United Nations 2002).

Following the MIPAA, the AU Policy Framework and Plan of Action on Ageing, which the African Union developed in 2003, aims to align the larger MIPAA goals with the unique African context (HelpAge International 2003). Historically, there has been some skepticism in the African context about Western LTC strategies (Aboderin and Ferreira 2008). Thus, policies in the AU Plan of Action on Ageing include infrastructure development that is rooted in African cultural values.

The AU Plan of Action on Ageing has three major strategies: multidimensional health promotion to prevent disease and disability among older people, implementation of policies to ensure unrestricted access to rehabilitation and curative care, and development of a workforce specialized in the care of older people (Saka, Oosthuizen, and Nlooto 2019). Both MIPAA and the AU Plan of Action on Ageing encourage countries to "mainstream" their LTC policies (Aboderin and Ferreira 2008) by organically integrating policies that support healthy aging across all adult age groups into larger plans related to socioeconomic development rather than targeting and isolating older persons as a distinct group.

Following the establishment of MIPAA and the AU Plan of Action on Ageing, several African countries have developed policies related to the elderly. Table 5.3 lists 17 African countries with legislation related to health care for older adults.

A few countries, including Mauritius, Seychelles, and South Africa, have developed some organized systems of long-term care. Even in these countries, significant gaps remain in the number of LTC facilities and other resources. In South Africa, the rights of persons receiving home-based and institutional care services are defined and protected by legislation through the 2006 Older Persons Act.

TABLE 5.3 Sub-Saharan African Countries with Health Care Legislation for Older People

Country	Legislation
Botswana	National Healthy Ageing Programme
Ethiopia	National Plan of Action on Older Persons
Ghana	National Policy on Older People
Kenya	National Policy on Older Persons and Ageing
Lesotho	Lesotho Policy for Older Persons
Malawi	National Policy for Older Persons
Mauritius	Ageing with Dignity
Mozambique	National Plan of Action for Older People
Namibia	National Pensions Act
Senegal	Sesame Plan
Seychelles	National Policy on Ageing
South Africa	Older Persons Act
Tanzania	National Ageing Policy
Uganda	National Plan of Action for Older People
Zambia	National Ageing Policy
Zimbabwe	Older Person Act

Sources: Saka, Oosthuizen, and Nlooto 2019. For a description of Mauritius' Ageing with Dignitity, refer to https://ifa.ngo/wp
-content/uploads/2012/11/060_21-Mauritius-2001-Ageing-With-Dignity-National-Policy-on-th.pdf. For a description of Senegal's
Sesame Plan, refer to Ka et al. 2016.

However, the qualification criteria for accessing these services can be quite stringent, and admission is not guaranteed.

A review of LTC policies in various African countries finds consistency in the provision of government financial support to help older people defray health care and LTC expenses (Aboderin 2019). Many of these policies, such as the Ageing with Dignity Program in Mauritius and the National Pensions Act in Namibia, attempt to provide older people with income security. In Kenya, the draft Older Persons of Society bill establishes the state's responsibility to care for persons 60 years and older by providing a universal cash transfer for LTC services, but not directly providing services (Aboderin 2019).

Family caregivers are nevertheless still expected to provide care—such as in-home services and respite care—for older family members, even though both the MIPAA and the AU Plan of Action on Ageing concede that, in the case of very frail or sick older persons, formal support may be a better option than informal family caregiving.

At the policy level, many policies that are not specific to older adults nonetheless affect them indirectly. For example, policies regarding health-related social needs such as housing development, clean water, and proper sanitation all have an impact on older adults (Indongo and Sakaria 2016). As the regional conversation around the increase of aging populations continues, some countries such as Senegal are prioritizing policies specific to health care for older adults. In Senegal, the Sesame Plan targets chronic pathologies often present in the older population by gathering data on geriatric disease trends and the current and future demography of older adults and by integrating health care in primary care facilities at multiple levels across rural and urban communities (Ka et al. 2016).

Key Challenges and Policy Considerations

Juggling Multipronged Challenges and Policy Priorities

In the foreseeable future, it is likely that policy makers in many African countries, which include 32 of the poorest countries, will continue to prioritize economic development and poverty alleviation as well as initiatives to expand health care access for all age groups over LTC issues for older adults. For example, a recent study of 56 lower-middle-income countries (including 34 countries in Sub-Saharan Africa) revealed that only one in five of the nonelderly survey participants reported having health insurance during the period 2006–18, and their associated countries did not have adequate universal health insurance coverage, if any at all (Chen et al. 2022). Thus, it would be reasonable and well justified for regional policy makers to prioritize the expansion of health care insurance to achieve universal health coverage.

Ultimately, policy makers in African countries will have to juggle multipronged challenges and priorities with limited resources. Proper sequencing of competing priorities will be important—in the African context, policy efforts to boost income security for older people and to expand basic health insurance for the whole population may be perceived as more urgent than providing long-term care for older adults with ADL disabilities. However, planning for and developing LTC services and the requisite policy frameworks should begin sooner rather than later, given the inevitable escalation of care needs among aging populations in the coming decades.

Supporting Family Caregiving

Family caregiving remains the bedrock of long-term care for older Africans and will continue to be so in the foreseeable future. Meanwhile, policy makers should identify the limitations of family-based long-term care, particularly in the care of older persons with severe functional impairments and complex conditions, and develop appropriate policies, services, and trainings to support family caregivers (Feng 2019). As an overarching policy goal, a mixed—and well-balanced—LTC system of informal and formal services is desirable. In light of the strong preference for home- and community-based care and the perceived stigma associated with institutional care in many African societies (Aboderin 2019), policy development and resource allocation should prioritize a care structure of LTC services that is based in older people's homes and in community settings.

The significant "hidden" costs and adverse impacts of informal care provision on family caregivers and society at large should be weighed adequately in the policy-making process. The lack of affordable formal LTC services to complement informal care for older adults results in enormous opportunity costs for working-age family caregivers, who are often forced to reduce their labor force participation or forgo employment altogether, resulting in forgone productivity both for themselves and for the economy. In African countries, as elsewhere in the world, women are disproportionately affected, as they are the primary family caregivers. To the extent that women are confined to caregiving duties and responsibilities in the home, their income-generating capacity and future financial security in old age will be negatively affected.

Taking an Incremental and Carefully Sequenced Approach to Developing Long-Term Care—Through Strengthening and Expanding Primary Health Care

Long-term care must build on existing health care systems and infrastructure. Specifically, policy makers should consider gradually adding and integrating appropriate types of LTC services in the existing primary health care settings. At the outset, basic services such as screening for chronic conditions, health risk and disability assessments, medication management, nursing care, and rehabilitation services could be offered.

Prevention strategies for noncommunicable diseases and the improvement of primary care will have positive effects on the health of older people and allow decision-makers to include LTC in larger public health goals (Ka et al. 2016). Significant efforts to expand and upgrade the health care and LTC workforce and to offer education and training to meet geriatric health care needs will be necessary to ensure success (Mussie et al. 2022). Workforce strengthening and improvement efforts should aim to reduce disparities in access to care between rural and urban areas. Finally, increased communication and collaboration through cross-country learning, both within Africa and with countries outside of the continent, would enhance the success of policies and initiatives to improve the health of older adults and support healthy aging and longevity.

References

Aboderin, Isabella. 2019. "Toward a Fit-for-Purpose Policy Architecture on Long-Term Care in Sub-Saharan Africa: Impasse and a Research Agenda to Overcome It." *Journal of Long-Term Care* (September 2019): 119–26. https://doi.org/10.31389/jltc.5.

Aboderin, Isabella, and Monica Ferreira. 2008. "Linking Ageing to Development Agendas in Sub-Saharan Africa: Challenges and Approaches." *Journal of Population Ageing* 1 (1): 51–73.

Chen, Simiao, Pascal Geldsetzer, Qiushi Chen, Mosa Moshabela, Lirui Jiao, Osondu Ogbuoji, Ali Sie, et al. 2022. "Health Insurance Coverage in Low- and Middle-Income Countries Remains Far from the Goal of Universal Coverage." *Health Affairs (Millwood)* 41 (8): 1142–52. https://doi.org/10.1377/hlthaff.2021.00951.

Feng, Zhanlian. 2019. "Global Convergence: Aging and Long-Term Care Policy Challenges in the Developing World." *Journal of Aging and Social Policy* 31 (4): 291–97. https://doi.org/10.1080/08959420.2019.1626205.

He, Wan, Isabella Aboderin, and Dzifa Adjaye-Gbewonyo. 2020. *Africa Aging: 2020.* Washington, DC: US Census Bureau.

HelpAge International. 2003. *AU Policy Framework and Plan of Action on Ageing.* Nairobi: HelpAge International, Africa Regional Development Centre.

Indongo, Nelago, and Nafal Sakaria. 2016. "Living Arrangements and Conditions of Older People in Namibia." *Advances in Aging Research* 5 (5): 97–109. https://doi.org/10.4236/aar.2016.55010.

Ka, O., M. M. M. Leye, G. Awa, P. G. Sow, A. Tal Dia, S. N. Diop, and A. M. Sow. 2016. "Towards a Geriatrics Policy Integrated to the Primary Health Cares in Africa (the Case of Senegal)." *Journal of Gerontology & Geriatric Research* 5 (1): 1000274. https://doi.org/10.4172/2167-7182.1000274.

Lloyd-Sherlock, Peter. 2014. "Beyond Neglect: Long-Term Care Research in Low and Middle Income Countries." *International Journal of Gerontology* 8 (2): 66–69.

Mussie, Kirubel M., Jenny Setchell, Bernice S. Elger, Mirgissa Kaba, Solomon T. Memirie, and Tenzin Wangmo. 2022. "Care of Older Persons in Eastern Africa: A Scoping Review of Ethical Issues." *Frontiers in Public Health* 10 (July 6, 2022): 923097. https://doi.org/10.3389/fpubh.2022.923097.

Saka, Sule, Frasia Oosthuizen, and Manimbulu Nlooto. 2019. "National Policies and Older People's Healthcare in Sub-Saharan Africa: A Scoping Review." *Annals of Global Health* 85 (1): 91. https://doi.org/10.5334/aogh.2401.

Scheil-Adlung, Xenia. 2015. "Long-Term Care Protection for Older Persons: A Review of Coverage Deficits in 46 Countries." ESS Working Paper 50, International Labour Office, Geneva.

Schneider, Luisa T. 2020. "Elders and Transactional Relationships in Sierra Leone: Rethinking Synchronic Approaches." *Africa* 90 (4): 701–20. https://doi.org/10.1017/S0001972020000285.

United Nations. 2002. *Political Declaration and Madrid International Plan of Action on Ageing.* New York: United Nations.

UN DESA (United Nations Department of Economic and Social Affairs). 2022. *World Population Prospects 2022* (online edition). New York: UN DESA, Population Division. https://population.un.org/wpp.

WHO (World Health Organization). 2017. *Towards Long-Term Care Systems in Sub-Saharan Africa.* Geneva: WHO.

CHAPTER 6

The Unmet Need: Assessing the Demand for and Supply of Home-Based Support for Older Adults with Disabilities in European Countries and Comparators

Yuting Qian, Shanquan Chen, Xiaohui Hou, Zhuoer Lin, Zexuan Yu, Mengxiao Wang, and Xi Chen

Key Messages

- Accurately assessing unmet care needs in older-adult populations is critical for effective response. This study quantifies care shortfalls among older adults with disabilities in 27 European countries and 4 global comparators between 2011 and 2018.

- During the period, many study countries experienced an increase in the prevalence of disability but a decrease in the percentage of older adults receiving assistance with their limitations—often because populations of older adults were growing quickly.

- The study shows substantial unmet older-adult care needs in most countries studied but also divergent results among countries at comparable income levels, suggesting important opportunities for peer learning and performance gains.

- Factors associated with the prevalence and severity of disability and with the receipt of assistance differ by country. However, in most settings, age, partner status, income, and education are significantly associated with functional limitations and differential receipt of care. Countries may improve outcomes by directing interventions to vulnerable groups of older adults with disabilities—for example, unpartnered men.

- The study underlines the importance of quantitative measurement and evaluation in identifying policy levers to strengthen older-adult care.

Introduction

The World Health Organization (WHO) estimates that, as of 2011, about 15 percent of the world's population had a disability. Although more recent estimates are not available, the evidence suggests that, as the global population becomes older, the levels of disability may be even higher. In the 2000s, the prevalence of disability among people ages 60 and older was 43.4 percent in low- and middle-income countries and 29.5 percent in high-income countries (WHO 2011).

A key way in which health systems measure disability—in particular, how well individuals can or cannot take care of themselves and live on their own—is to document the individual's capacity to perform activities of daily living (ADLs) and instrumental activities of daily living (IADLs) (Kiyoshige et al. 2019; NRC Committee on National Statistics and NRC Committee on Population 2009).[1]

Assistance with daily living is essential for adults with ADL/IADL limitations. The need for nursing-home placement and health care use can also be predicted by ADL/IADL limitations (Covinsky 2006; Mor et al. 1994). In particular, older adults with disabilities need more long-term care and hospitalization, and they face higher health care costs, a lower quality of life, and an increased risk of death (Choi and Schoeni 2017; Loyd et al. 2020; Sengupta et al. 2018). ADL/IADL limitations therefore impose a heavy burden on individuals, families, and health systems. During the COVID-19 pandemic, ADL/IADL limitations brought even greater challenges for persons with disabilities and their families, including increased risks for low psychological well-being and poor quality of life (Steptoe and Di Gessa 2021).

This study (a) documents the characteristics of individuals with ADL and IADL limitations and estimates the prevalence of these disabilities over time in multiple countries; (b) evaluates the extent to which the needs of older adults with disabilities are not being met and how this situation is changing over time; and (c) analyzes the factors that contribute to the gap between the demand for care from, and the supply of care to, older people with ADL/IADL limitations.

Study Design and Target Populations

The study employs a consistent time period for comparison across all of the surveys consulted: the English Longitudinal Survey on Ageing; the Survey of Health, Ageing, and Retirement in Europe; the Health and Retirement Study; and the China Health and Retirement Longitudinal Study. The study includes 31 countries, including China, Israel, the United Kingdom, the United States, and 27 European countries (Austria, Belgium, Bulgaria, Croatia, Cyprus, Czechia, Denmark, Estonia, Finland, France, Germany, Greece, Hungary, Italy, Latvia, Lithuania, Luxembourg, Malta, the Netherlands, Poland, Portugal, Romania, the Slovak Republic, Slovenia, Spain, Sweden, and Switzerland). Outcome variables are limitations in relation to six basic activities of daily living and five instrumental activities of daily living. The ADLs include dressing, walking across a room, bathing, eating, getting in and out of bed, and toileting; the

IADLs include preparing a hot meal, shopping for groceries, making phone calls, taking medications, and managing money (Bousquet et al. 2020; Edwards et al. 2020; Jang, Ko, and Han 2021). The second outcome variable is the receipt of assistance with ADL/IADL limitations.

Key Findings

The longitudinal samples of four waves across all countries include a total of 470,057 person-waves. The sample size, mean age, and share of respondents who are women, by country, in each wave are presented in table 6A.1. Within the sample, on average, during the study period, Lithuania had the highest proportion of women respondents (64.1 percent), while China had the lowest share of women respondents (52.4 percent). On average, during the study period, the mean age of surveyed adults was highest in Sweden (69.7 years) and lowest in China (59.6 years).

On average, all the European Union (EU) countries had a lower prevalence of ADL/IADL limitations over the period—15.8 percent in 2011 and 15.4 percent in 2017—than China (25.8 percent in 2011 and 30.4 percent in 2018), the United States (25.0 percent in 2012 and 24.9 percent in 2018), or the United Kingdom (21.4 percent in 2012 and 20.4 percent in 2018) (table 6A.2). Table 6A.2 shows that the average extent of ADL/IADL limitations was higher in the European Union than in China or the United Kingdom, but lower than in the United States. The average extent of ADL/IADL limitations was at 2.94 in 2011 and 3.18 in 2017 in the European Union, 2.92 in 2012 and 3.13 in 2018 in the United Kingdom, 2.76 in 2011 and 3.09 in 2018 in China, and 3.43 in 2012 and 3.22 in 2018 in the United States.

Trends in the Prevalence of ADL/IADL Limitations

In-country trends in the prevalence of ADL/IADL limitations are inconsistent throughout the study period. By comparing the prevalence in ADL/IADL limitations in the first year and last year of the study period, the trend in prevalence of ADL/IADL limitations was generally decreasing for 10 countries: Estonia, Germany, Greece, Hungary, Luxembourg, the Netherlands, Poland, Sweden, the United Kingdom, and the United States. The trend in 13 other countries—Austria, Belgium, China, Croatia, Czechia, Denmark, France, Israel, Italy, Portugal, Slovenia, Spain, and Switzerland—was generally increasing (figure 6.1).

In addition, in some cases, there is heterogeneity in time trends between ADL and IADL limitations. For example, Greece experienced a decline in the prevalence of ADL limitations, but an increase in the presence of IADL limitations. China had the highest prevalence of ADL/IADL limitations, while Switzerland had the lowest prevalence of ADL/IADL limitations in both the baseline year of the study (2011/12) and the final year (2017/18).

The prevalence of ADL/IADL limitations varies substantially among countries over the years, with some countries changing their rankings compared with others. For example, Germany had a lower prevalence of ADL/IADL limitations than Luxembourg in 2013, but a higher prevalence in 2017.

FIGURE 6.1 Country-Specific Trends in the Prevalence of ADL/IADL Limitations, 2011–18

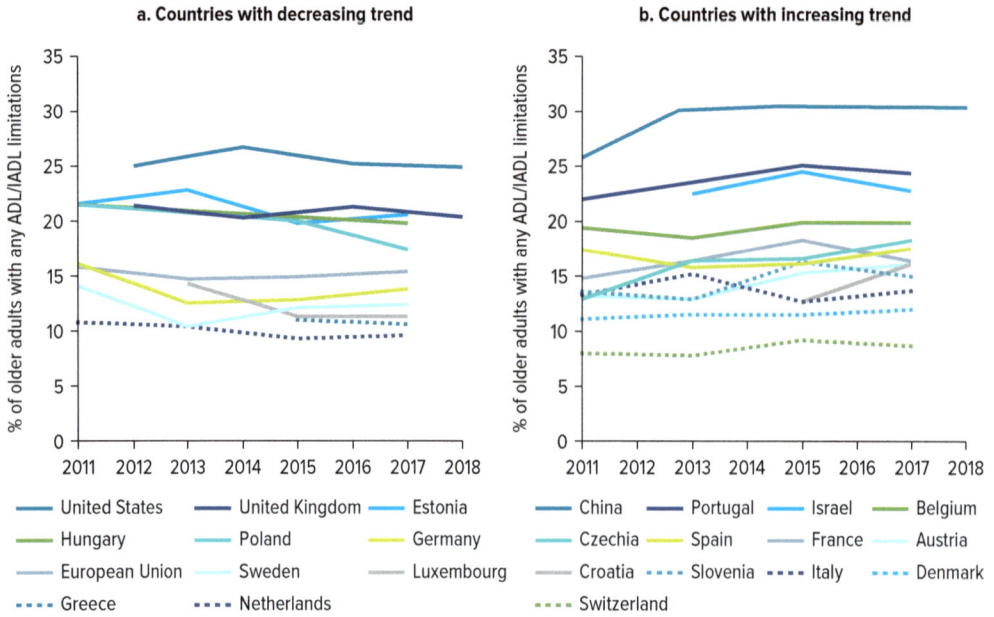

Source: Calculations based on data from the English Longitudinal Survey on Ageing; the Survey of Health, Ageing, and Retirement in Europe; the Health and Retirement Survey; and the China Health and Retirement Longitudinal Study.
Note: ADL = activities of daily living; IADL = instrumental activities of daily living.

Trends in the Extent of ADL/IADL Limitations

To gauge older people's quality of life and address their care needs, decision-makers and policy or program implementers need to know not just whether older adults have disabilities but how severe their disabilities are (figure 6.2). Switzerland had the lowest average extent of ADL/IADL limitations in both 2011/12 (2.04) and 2017/18 (2.19). Spain had the highest average extent of ADL/IADL limitations in both years: 4.70 in 2011 and 4.55 in 2017.

The trends in the extent of limitations are similarly inconsistent across countries. In every country, the mean extent of ADL/IADL limitations underwent fluctuations and changes. In seven countries—Germany, Greece, Luxembourg, the Netherlands, Poland, Sweden, and the United States—both the prevalence and the mean extent of ADL/IADL limitations decreased. In nine countries—Austria, Belgium, China, Czechia, France, Italy, Portugal, Slovenia, and Switzerland—both the prevalence and the mean extent of ADL/IADL limitations increased. In some countries, such as the United Kingdom, the prevalence of ADL/IADL limitations decreased, but the mean extent increased, indicating that older adults experienced fewer disabilities, but the disabilities they did experience were more severe.

FIGURE 6.2 Country-Specific Trends in the Mean Extent of ADL/IADL Limitations, 2011–18

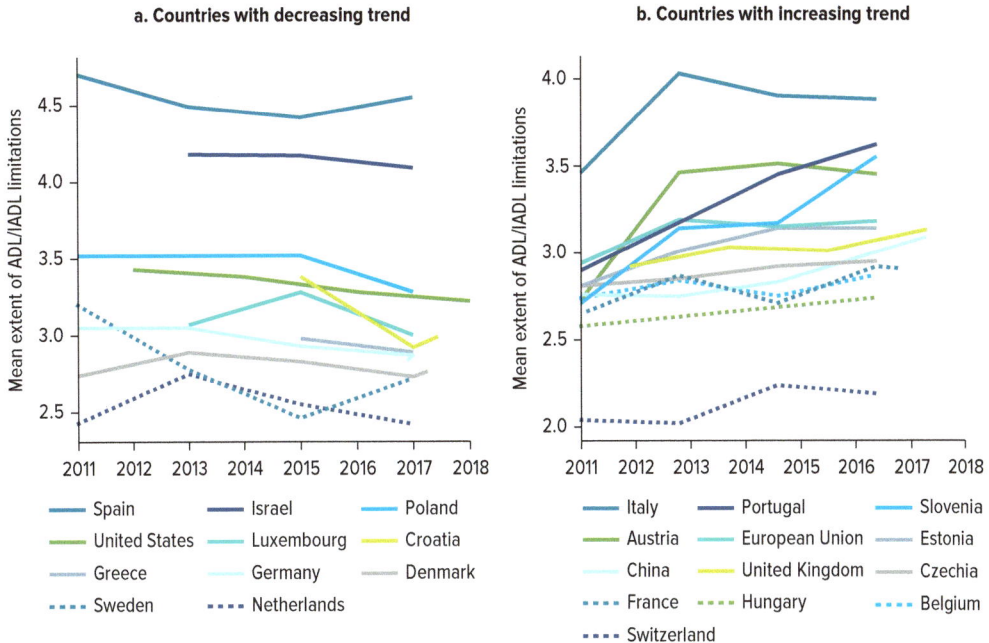

Source: Calculations based on data from the English Longitudinal Survey on Ageing; the Survey of Health, Ageing, and Retirement in Europe; the Health and Retirement Study; and the China Health and Retirement Longitudinal Study.
Note: ADL = activities of daily living; IADL = instrumental activities of daily living.

Cross-Country Trends in Receipt of Help for ADL/IADL Limitations

In most countries, with the exception of Israel, Switzerland, and the United Kingdom, the percentage of older adults receiving assistance for ADL/IADL limitations decreased (figure 6.3). On average, the European Union had a lower proportion of individuals with ADL/IADL limitations receiving assistance than China, the United Kingdom, and the United States (table 6A.2). The percentage of individuals with ADL/IADL limitations receiving assistance was 38.7 percent in 2013 and 23.4 percent in 2017 in the European Union, 62.4 percent in 2013 and 61.5 percent in 2018 in China, 65.6 percent in 2012 and 63.3 percent in 2018 in the United States, and 58.3 percent in 2012 and 59.2 percent in 2018 in the United Kingdom.

Health Expenditure and ADL/IADL Limitations

A weak negative relationship exists between health expenditure per capita and both the prevalence and the extent of ADL/IADL limitations among older adults. As a result, the relationship between increased health expenditure per capita and reduced prevalence and severity of ADL/IADL limitations among older adults is not straightforward. In this study, older adults in countries with

FIGURE 6.3 Percentage of Older Adults with ADL/IADL Limitations Receiving Assistance

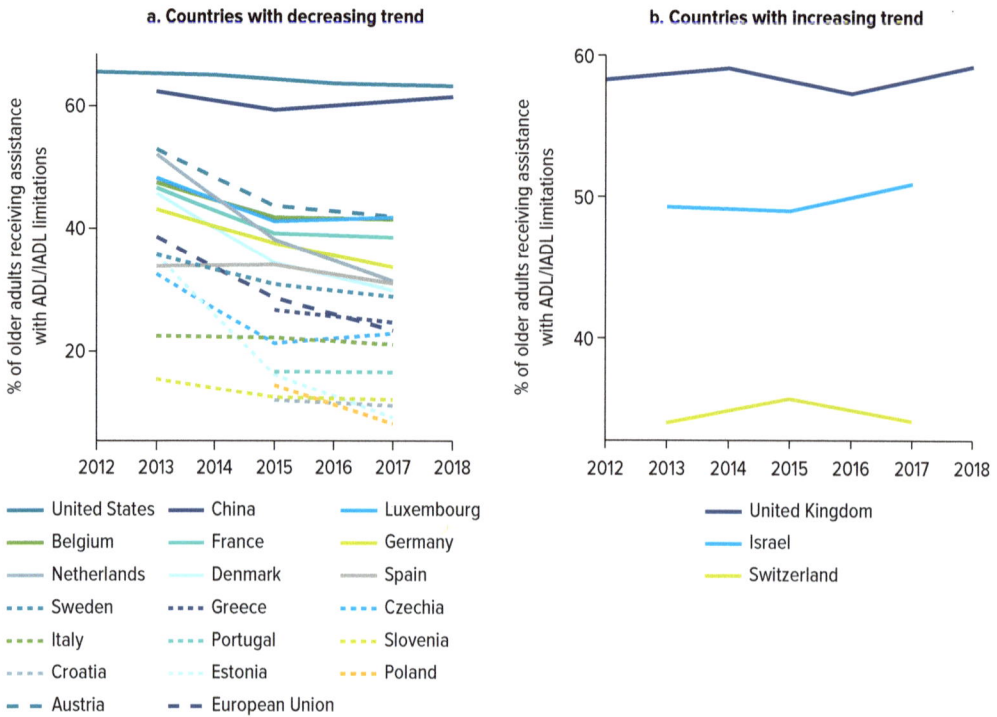

Source: Calculations based on data from the English Longitudinal Survey on Ageing; the Survey of Health, Ageing, and Retirement in Europe; the Health and Retirement Study; and the China Health and Retirement Longitudinal Study.
Note: ADL = activities of daily living; IADL = instrumental activities of daily living.

similar levels of health expenditure per capita have significantly different disability profiles. As shown in figure 6.4, the mean prevalence and extent of ADL/IADL limitations among 19 countries with mean health expenditure per capita below US$3,500 vary widely. China had the highest mean prevalence of ADL/IADL limitations, at 29.2 percent, while Spain had the highest mean extent of ADL/IADL limitations, at 4.5. The Slovak Republic had both the lowest mean prevalence and lowest extent, at 7.6 percent and 2.0, respectively. These findings suggest that, while health expenditure per capita is a contributing factor, it is not the only factor—and perhaps not even the most critical one—that affects the prevalence and severity of ADL/IADL limitations among older adults.

Of the 10 countries with mean health expenditure per capita between US$3,500 and US$7,000, Belgium had the highest mean prevalence of ADL/IADL limitations, at 19.4 percent in 2011, while Austria had the highest mean extent, at 2.73 in 2011. Conversely, the Netherlands had the lowest mean prevalence of ADL/IADL limitations, at 9.3 percent in 2015, and Finland had the lowest mean extent, at 2.2 in 2017. These findings indicate that, even within the same range of health expenditure per capita, differences in the prevalence and severity of ADL/IADL limitations among older adults can be substantial.

FIGURE 6.4 Mean Prevalence and Extent of ADL/IADL Limitations in Relation to Mean Health Expenditure per Capita

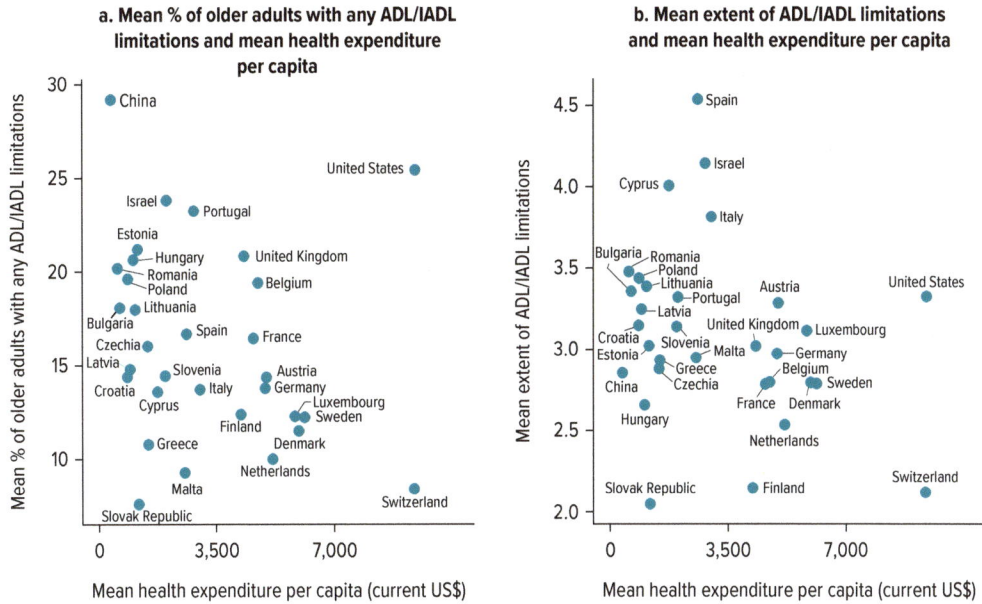

a. Mean % of older adults with any ADL/IADL limitations and mean health expenditure per capita

b. Mean extent of ADL/IADL limitations and mean health expenditure per capita

Source: Calculations based on data from the English Longitudinal Survey on Ageing; the Survey of Health, Ageing, and Retirement in Europe; the Health and Retirement Study; and the China Health and Retirement Longitudinal Study.
Note: ADL = activities of daily living; IADL = instrumental activities of daily living.

Unadjusted Annual Percentage Change in ADL/IADL Limitations and in the Receipt of Assistance

Current systems for delivering care to older adults with disabilities are inadequate and struggling to meet the growing demand. Using annual percentage change to measure the trends of ADL/IADL limitation, the results indicate that, over the study period, 15 countries experienced a decrease in the prevalence of ADL/IADL limitations, while 8 countries experienced an increase. Among the countries that experienced a decline in the prevalence of ADL/IADL limitations, Greece, Hungary, Israel, and Luxembourg had particularly high levels of decline, with annual percentage changes of –3.02 percent, –1.24 percent, –1.58 percent, and –2.32 percent, respectively. In contrast, Croatia had a significant increase in the prevalence of ADL/IADL limitations, with an annual percentage change of 3.09 percent.

Trends in the extent of ADL/IADL limitations also vary across the countries. In China, the United Kingdom, and most EU countries, including Austria, Czechia, Denmark, Estonia, France, Germany, Italy, the Netherlands, Portugal, Slovenia, and Switzerland, the extent of ADL/IADL limitations increased, with positive annual percentage changes ranging from 0.03 percent in Denmark to 0.89 percent in the Netherlands. However, some EU countries, such as Greece and Croatia, showed a decreasing trend, with negative annual percentage changes of –1.76 percent and –3.66 percent, respectively.

Most countries experienced a decline in the share of older adults receiving assistance, with the exception of China, Israel, Italy, Spain, and the United Kingdom (figure 6.5). The annual percentage change in the provision of assistance for older adults with ADL/IADL limitations ranges from –10 to 0 for most countries.

FIGURE 6.5 Unadjusted Annual Percentage Change in ADL/IADL Limitations and Receipt of Assistance

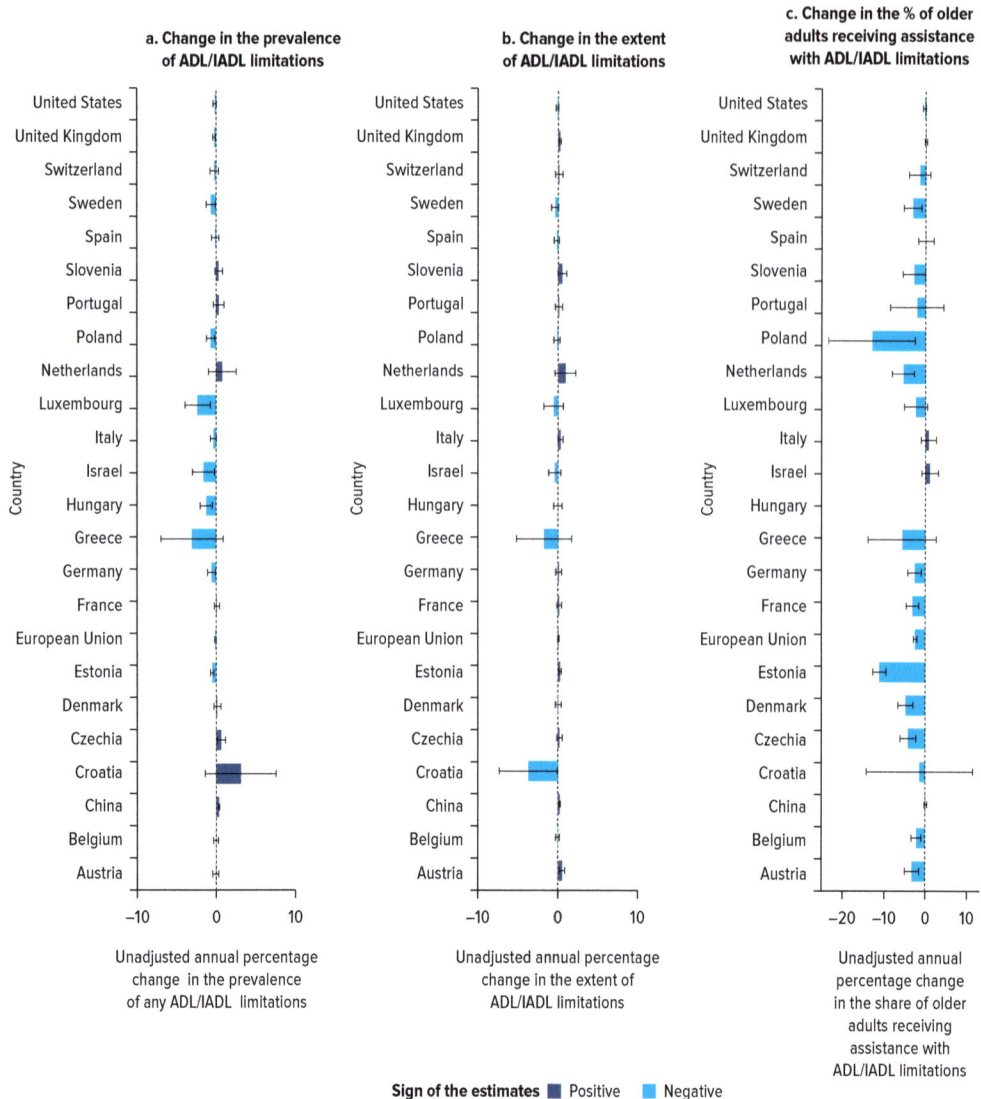

Source: Calculations based on data from the English Longitudinal Survey on Ageing; the Survey of Health, Ageing, and Retirement in Europe; the Health and Retirement Study; and the China Health and Retirement Longitudinal Study.
Note: ADL = activities of daily living; IADL = instrumental activities of daily living.

In five countries—Estonia, the Netherlands, Poland, Portugal, and Slovenia—the annual percentage change in the receipt of assistance was high and negative, while the demand by older adults for assistance with ADL/IADL limitations was either stable or increasing, as indicated by a positive or slightly negative annual percentage change. A gap appears to be growing between the need for and provision of assistance with daily life tasks among older adults in these countries.

Predictors of ADL/IADL Limitations

A wide range of demographic, socioeconomic, epidemiologic, and policy factors may influence the prevalence and severity of disabilities in aging populations. In all 31 countries except for Cyprus, Finland, and France, older age is significantly associated with an increased risk of ADL/IADL limitations over the study period. In 20 countries, older age is also significantly associated with an increased risk of more extensive ADL/IADL limitations.[2]

In nearly half of the countries studied, having a partner and a higher income is associated with a lower risk of onset of ADL/IADL limitations. However, in some countries, the relationship between these factors and the severity of ADL/IADL limitations is inconsistent. For example, in the United Kingdom, individuals in the highest income quintile had a lower average severity of ADL/IADL limitations, while in Cyprus, they had a higher average severity of disability.[3]

In 20 countries, education has a consistent and significant negative relationship with the prevalence of ADL/IADL limitations. This result indicates that a higher level of education is associated with a lower risk of disability in later life. In 10 countries, education is also found to have a significant negative relationship with the extent of ADL/IADL limitations, meaning that better-educated individuals experience less severe disability in old age.

In a limited number of the countries studied, the prevalence and extent of ADL/IADL limitations are also influenced by factors such as sex, number of children, and retirement status. However, the relationship between these factors and the prevalence or extent of limitations is inconsistent, with both positive and negative associations observed across countries.

Predictors of Older Adults Receiving Assistance with ADL/IADL Limitations

In several countries, sex, number of children, and retirement status are also found to influence the likelihood of receiving assistance for ADL/IADL limitations. However, these associations vary from country to country and are not consistent across countries. In most countries, education is positively associated with the receipt of assistance, but in Poland, Slovenia, and the United States, better-educated individuals are less likely to receive help.

Discussion

These findings have important implications for the provision of health care services and indicate the need for support and assistance for older adults with ADL/IADL limitations. The rising trend of ADL/IADL limitations in several countries highlights the need to pay attention and prepare to address the future burden of increasing later-life disabilities and the increasing demand for formal and informal care.

The results show that there is a decreasing trend in the share of disabled older adults receiving assistance. A recent study suggests that the provision of ADL assistance is positively associated with the level of national welfare support (Chen et al. 2022). However, the reason for the decreasing trend is not clear. The significant decline in assistance received for ADL/IADL limitations, especially compared with the increasing trend in ADL/IADL limitations in some countries, highlights the unmet need for ADL/IADL assistance among older adults.

In Croatia and Greece, the decline in assistance received for ADL/IADL limitations may be linked to a high decline in the prevalence and extent of ADL/IADL limitations. However, in many other EU countries (Austria, Belgium, Czechia, Denmark, Estonia, France, Germany, Luxembourg, the Netherlands, Poland, Slovenia, and Sweden), where the prevalence of ADL/IADL limitations is either declining only slightly or is even increasing, the findings suggest potential substantial unmet needs for disabled older people. These countries may benefit from expanding social care services and creating a more integrated health and social care system. Such an expansion, coupled with more integration, would provide better care services and reduce unmet needs among older people with disabilities.

Many of this study's findings—such as that factors including age, partner status, income, and education have a significant impact on the prevalence and extent of ADL/IADL limitations in multiple countries—are in line with prior research suggesting that socioeconomic status plays a significant role in the prevalence, extent, and receipt of assistance for disability among older adults (Liu and Wang 2022). In Belgium, France, Israel, Italy, the Netherlands, the United Kingdom, and the United States, older seniors and women are more likely to receive help with ADL/IADL limitations. These countries may be able to improve outcomes for older adults with disabilities by targeting support to particularly vulnerable groups, including younger seniors and men. Improving the availability and uptake of both informal care and formal services among these vulnerable groups may help to reduce the unmet needs of older adults.

Demographic and socioeconomic factors, such as age, partner status, income, and education, are significant predictors of ADL/IADL limitations and the receipt of help. However, the association between these factors and the receipt of assistance is country-specific. For example, older adults without partners are less likely to receive assistance with ADL/IADL limitations in China, but this association is not statistically significant in several EU countries: Bulgaria, Croatia, Czechia, Poland, the Slovak Republic, and Slovenia. The difference may be due to differences in the model of care provision adopted in China and in EU countries. In China, spouses are the most common caregiver for disabled older adults requiring care. By contrast, in Europe, care is often provided in various forms of long-term care facilities, along with a greater provision of public services and formal care, which likely weakens the role of partners in predicting the probability of receiving care with ADL/IADL limitations (Li and Dai 2018; Solé-Auró and Crimmins 2014).

The country-to-country variations in unmet needs may be attributed to differences in the number and types of services and welfare models used. The availability and quality of long-term care services also vary greatly between countries and can have a significant impact on the prevalence of ADL/IADL limitations and the receipt of care for persons with limitations. It is important to consider the interplay between health care and social services in addressing unmet care needs among disabled older people (Anderson and Knickman 2001; Arnaert, Van Den Heuvel, and Windey 2005; Bien et al. 2013). In the United States in recent decades, social and economic inequalities have widened sharply, while publicly funded health care and social welfare programs remain more limited than in other high-income countries (Banks et al. 2006; Case and Deaton 2020; Schneider et al. 2021). Cultural norms and beliefs surrounding aging and caregiving also play a role in explaining the cross-country variations in ADL/IADL limitations and the availability of care for older adults. Further research is needed to understand the factors driving these cross-country differences and to develop targeted, evidence-based interventions to address the growing burden of ADL/IADL limitations and care needs for older adults.

Overall, these findings underscore a significant gap in many countries between the demand for support by older adults with ADL/IADL limitations and the insufficient availability of care for these adults. Yet the results also point to opportunities for learning and policy actions that could improve outcomes. The observed cross-country variations, together with the contributing demographic and socioeconomic factors identified in each country, can help guide countries that are experiencing a high prevalence or extent of ADL/IADL limitations and a high level of unmet need for disability support to launch or expand interventions targeted toward high-risk older adults. Opportunities and best practices exist for countries to learn from comparable peer nations that have faced similar challenges and successfully improved their care results for older citizens with disabilities.

Annex 6A Supplementary Tables

TABLE 6A.1 Descriptive Analysis of the Sample, by Age and Sex, Various Years, 2011–18

Country	Year	Number	Mean age (SE)	Women (%)
Austria	2011	5,134	65.14 (10.23)	58.1
Austria	2013	4,279	66.68 (10.02)	57.6
Austria	2015	3,323	68.73 (9.77)	58.4
Austria	2017	3,176	70.25 (9.47)	59.2
Belgium	2011	5,322	64.45 (10.98)	55.4
Belgium	2013	5,635	65.33 (10.88)	55.4
Belgium	2015	5,814	65.78 (11.01)	55.8
Belgium	2017	4,900	67.54 (10.44)	55.7
Bulgaria	2017	1,998	65.90 (10.01)	58.2
China	2011	17,708	58.50 (10.17)	52.1

(continued)

TABLE 6A.1 Descriptive Analysis of the Sample, by Age and Sex, Various Years, 2011–18 *(continued)*

Country	Year	Number	Mean age (SE)	Women (%)
China	2013	18,612	59.41 (10.29)	52.3
China	2015	21,097	59.09 (10.75)	52.3
China	2018	19,816	61.44 (10.41)	52.9
Croatia	2015	2,495	64.71 (9.61)	56.0
Croatia	2017	2,408	65.88 (9.27)	55.8
Cyprus	2017	1,233	68.58 (10.88)	59.9
Czechia	2011	5,523	64.89 (9.75)	58.5
Czechia	2013	5,635	66.20 (9.43)	58.9
Czechia	2015	4,851	67.66 (9.09)	59.8
Czechia	2017	4,212	69.65 (8.76)	60.1
Denmark	2011	2,287	64.15 (10.88)	54.5
Denmark	2013	4,146	64.67 (10.39)	54.1
Denmark	2015	3,733	65.05 (10.32)	54.0
Denmark	2017	3,246	66.48 (9.83)	54.4
Estonia	2011	6,863	65.84 (10.28)	59.7
Estonia	2013	5,751	67.69 (9.94)	60.4
Estonia	2015	5,638	67.64 (10.71)	60.8
Estonia	2017	5,115	69.13 (10.37)	61.4
Finland	2017	2,007	65.62 (9.86)	54.1
France	2011	5,850	65.22 (11.23)	57.3
France	2013	4,505	66.98 (10.68)	57.4
France	2015	3,947	67.29 (11.08)	57.4
France	2017	3,331	68.84 (10.5)	58.3
Germany	2011	1,619	67.75 (8.91)	53.3
Germany	2013	5,750	64.00 (10.33)	53.2
Germany	2015	4,411	65.81 (9.89)	52.9
Germany	2017	3,820	67.37 (9.47)	53.2
Greece	2015	4,924	66.50 (10.56)	56.9
Greece	2017	3,070	69.14 (9.58)	57.8
Hungary	2011	3,072	64.17 (9.81)	57.1
Hungary	2017	1,538	68.58 (8.24)	60.5
Israel	2013	2,599	67.36 (10.42)	56.3
Israel	2015	2,035	69.64 (10.15)	57.8
Israel	2017	2,131	70.26 (9.65)	57.5
Italy	2011	3,568	66.19 (9.86)	55.2
Italy	2013	4,739	66.4 (10.22)	55.1

(continued)

TABLE 6A.1 Descriptive Analysis of the Sample, by Age and Sex, Various Years, 2011–18 *(continued)*

Country	Year	Number	Mean age (SE)	Women (%)
Italy	2015	5,305	66.56 (10.20)	54.9
Italy	2017	4,568	68.40 (9.88)	55.1
Latvia	2017	1,734	66.28 (10.85)	63.6
Lithuania	2017	2,035	65.77 (10.83)	64.1
Luxembourg	2013	1,607	64.34 (9.96)	53.1
Luxembourg	2015	1,563	64.55 (9.66)	54.7
Luxembourg	2017	1,250	66.16 (9.22)	54.2
Malta	2017	1,261	66.46 (9.29)	56.2
Netherlands	2011	2,788	65.32 (9.79)	55.9
Netherlands	2013	4,165	65.70 (9.87)	55.4
Netherlands	2015	4,575	65.66 (8.89)	52.2
Netherlands	2017	4,090	66.95 (8.28)	51.9
Poland	2011	1,733	66.63 (9.27)	56.4
Poland	2015	1,826	66.01 (10.02)	56.6
Poland	2017	4,703	65.49 (10.05)	55.5
Portugal	2011	2,013	64.28 (10.02)	57.2
Portugal	2015	1,674	67.04 (9.15)	55.1
Portugal	2017	1,282	69.69 (8.75)	55.9
Romania	2017	2,114	64.89 (9.77)	57.5
Slovak Republic	2017	2,077	61.43 (8.55)	54.2
Slovenia	2011	2,748	64.96 (10.22)	56.6
Slovenia	2013	2,958	66.19 (10.20)	57.1
Slovenia	2015	4,223	67.04 (9.82)	57.1
Slovenia	2017	3,691	68.71 (9.46)	58.1
Spain	2011	3,727	67.30 (11.19)	55.3
Spain	2013	6,693	67.75 (11.24)	54.3
Spain	2015	5,615	69.52 (10.83)	55.4
Spain	2017	4,704	70.93 (10.51)	56.0
Sweden	2011	1,969	69.46 (9.21)	54.3
Sweden	2013	4,555	68.00 (9.54)	53.5
Sweden	2015	3,905	69.78 (9.38)	54.3
Sweden	2017	3,196	71.55 (9.00)	54.0
Switzerland	2011	3,784	64.50 (10.51)	55.2
Switzerland	2013	3,048	66.03 (10.04)	55.2
Switzerland	2015	2,803	67.91 (9.85)	55.1
Switzerland	2017	2,402	69.53 (9.58)	54.8

(continued)

TABLE 6A.1 Descriptive Analysis of the Sample, by Age and Sex, Various Years, 2011–18 *(continued)*

Country	Year	Number	Mean age (SE)	Women (%)
European Union	2011	58,000	65.45 (10.38)	56.7
European Union	2013	63,466	66.27 (10.33)	55.9
European Union	2015	70,625	66.99 (10.22)	56.1
European Union	2017	79,161	67.89 (9.94)	56.8
United Kingdom	2012	10,601	66.48 (10.20)	55.2
United Kingdom	2014	9,666	67.30 (10.15)	55.5
United Kingdom	2016	8,445	68.85 (9.58)	55.6
United Kingdom	2018	8,736	67.82 (10.68)	55.9
United States	2012	20,554	66.85 (11.59)	58.5
United States	2014	18,747	67.90 (11.26)	58.9
United States	2016	20,912	65.70 (11.79)	58.6
United States	2018	17,146	67.00 (11.40)	59.0

Source: Calculations based on data from the English Longitudinal Survey on Ageing; the Survey of Health, Ageing, and Retirement in Europe; the Health and Retirement Study; and the China Health and Retirement Longitudinal Study.
Note: ADL = activities of daily living; IADL = instrumental activities of daily living; SE = standard error.

TABLE 6A.2 Descriptive Analysis of the Prevalence and Extent of ADL/IADL Limitations and Assistance Received, Various Years, 2011–18

Country	Year	ADL limitations		IADL limitations		Any ADL and IADL limitations		
		Prevalence (%)	Extent (mean (SE))	Prevalence (%)	Extent (mean (SE))	Prevalence (%)	Extent (mean (SE))	Assistance received (%)
Austria	2011	10.0	2.07 (1.51)	8.1	1.90 (1.23)	13.2	2.73 (2.50)	—
Austria	2013	10.2	2.33 (1.65)	8.9	2.34 (1.46)	12.9	3.46 (3.00)	53.0
Austria	2015	11.3	2.46 (1.77)	11.1	2.34 (1.46)	15.3	3.51 (3.16)	43.7
Austria	2017	12.1	2.39 (1.79)	11.3	2.34 (1.46)	16.1	3.45 (3.09)	42.0
Belgium	2011	15.7	1.95 (1.42)	11.2	2.01 (1.34)	19.4	2.74 (2.51)	—
Belgium	2013	15.4	1.99 (1.43)	10.7	2.05 (1.31)	18.5	2.84 (2.55)	47.5
Belgium	2015	15.8	1.97 (1.42)	11.6	2.02 (1.29)	19.9	2.75 (2.47)	41.8
Belgium	2017	15.5	2.07 (1.52)	12.1	2.05 (1.30)	19.9	2.87 (2.59)	41.5
Bulgaria	2017	13.8	2.47 (1.71)	12.8	2.10 (1.35)	18.1	3.36 (2.89)	12.7
China	2011	15.7	2.12 (1.40)	19.9	1.90 (1.06)	25.8	2.76 (2.26)	—
China	2013	17.8	2.11 (1.47)	23.4	1.93 (1.22)	30.1	2.75 (2.42)	62.4
China	2015	19.6	2.15 (1.49)	22.8	1.94 (1.23)	30.5	2.83 (2.47)	59.4
China	2018	19.7	2.28 (1.58)	23.8	2.06 (1.31)	30.4	3.09 (2.64)	61.5

(continued)

TABLE 6A.2 Descriptive Analysis of the Prevalence and Extent of ADL/IADL Limitations and Assistance Received, Various Years, 2011–18 *(continued)*

		ADL limitations		IADL limitations		Any ADL and IADL limitations		
Country	Year	Prevalence (%)	Extent (mean (SE))	Prevalence (%)	Extent (mean (SE))	Prevalence (%)	Extent (mean (SE))	Assistance received (%)
Croatia	2015	10.2	2.34 (1.70)	7.8	2.44 (1.42)	12.7	3.38 (2.96)	12.0
Croatia	2017	12.3	2.10 (1.51)	9.4	2.24 (1.38)	16.1	2.92 (2.63)	11.1
Cyprus	2017	8.3	2.97 (1.91)	12.0	2.50 (1.58)	13.6	4.01 (3.48)	54.2
Czechia	2011	9.7	2.06 (1.42)	8.0	2.03 (1.36)	12.9	2.81 (2.46)	—
Czechia	2013	13.0	2.09 (1.46)	9.4	2.09 (1.35)	16.4	2.85 (2.53)	32.6
Czechia	2015	13.6	2.14 (1.44)	9.3	2.09 (1.35)	16.6	2.92 (2.54)	21.3
Czechia	2017	14.6	2.10 (1.56)	10.8	2.17 (1.38)	18.3	2.95 (2.72)	22.9
Denmark	2011	7.7	1.91 (1.43)	7.4	2.10 (1.34)	11.1	2.74 (2.41)	—
Denmark	2013	8.6	2.03 (1.44)	7.2	2.18 (1.38)	11.5	2.89 (2.59)	45.8
Denmark	2015	8.2	2.11 (1.51)	7.5	2.05 (1.36)	11.5	2.83 (2.57)	34.4
Denmark	2017	8.4	2.10 (1.61)	7.6	1.97 (1.30)	12.0	2.73 (2.62)	29.9
Estonia	2011	16.7	2.10 (1.44)	13.0	1.97 (1.20)	21.6	2.81 (2.40)	—
Estonia	2013	17.5	2.21 (1.46)	14.6	2.06 (1.28)	22.8	3.01 (2.52)	35.8
Estonia	2015	15.0	2.24 (1.53)	13.0	2.19 (1.32)	19.8	3.14 (2.63)	16.2
Estonia	2017	15.4	2.25 (1.48)	14.0	2.13 (1.30)	20.6	3.14 (2.55)	9.2
Finland	2017	9.6	1.70 (1.11)	5.7	1.82 (1.18)	12.4	2.15 (1.94)	21.0
France	2011	11.7	1.94 (1.43)	8.5	1.97 (1.36)	14.8	2.65 (2.49)	—
France	2013	13.0	2.01 (1.49)	10.1	2.09 (1.42)	16.4	2.87 (2.66)	46.7
France	2015	14.5	1.95 (1.47)	10.7	1.99 (1.38)	18.3	2.71 (2.62)	39.2
France	2017	12.5	2.10 (1.61)	10.0	2.17 (1.48)	16.4	2.92 (2.82)	38.6
Germany	2011	13.8	2.26 (1.63)	8.9	2.01 (1.32)	16.1	3.05 (2.79)	—
Germany	2013	10.3	2.18 (1.50)	7.0	2.19 (1.38)	12.5	3.05 (2.67)	43.2
Germany	2015	10.7	2.11 (1.50)	7.1	2.07 (1.37)	12.8	2.93 (2.60)	37.6
Germany	2017	11.7	2.04 (1.47)	7.5	2.09 (1.38)	13.8	2.87 (2.60)	33.7
Greece	2015	7.8	2.25 (1.65)	7.8	1.97 (1.35)	11.0	2.98 (2.75)	26.7
Greece	2017	6.6	2.36 (1.67)	8.0	1.86 (1.29)	10.6	2.89 (2.79)	24.7
Hungary	2011	13.0	2.08 (1.37)	16.2	1.77 (1.14)	21.5	2.58 (2.20)	—
Hungary	2017	11.1	2.39 (1.71)	16.6	1.67 (1.11)	19.8	2.74 (2.50)	21.3
Israel	2013	13.6	3.26 (1.89)	20.0	2.47 (1.44)	22.5	4.18 (3.34)	49.3
Israel	2015	15.8	3.16 (1.91)	21.6	2.41 (1.38)	24.5	4.17 (3.29)	49.0
Israel	2017	12.7	3.28 (1.93)	21.3	2.43 (1.36)	22.8	4.09 (3.29)	50.9
Italy	2011	10.8	2.33 (1.69)	9.0	2.31 (1.53)	13.3	3.46 (3.06)	—
Italy	2013	12.9	2.66 (1.93)	9.8	2.76 (1.63)	15.2	4.03 (3.56)	22.5
Italy	2015	10.4	2.61 (1.81)	8.5	2.61 (1.63)	12.7	3.90 (3.37)	22.2

(continued)

TABLE 6A.2 Descriptive Analysis of the Prevalence and Extent of ADL/IADL Limitations and Assistance Received, Various Years, 2011–18 *(continued)*

Country	Year	ADL limitations		IADL limitations		Any ADL and IADL limitations		
		Prevalence (%)	Extent (mean (SE))	Prevalence (%)	Extent (mean (SE))	Prevalence (%)	Extent (mean (SE))	Assistance received (%)
Italy	2017	10.1	2.73 (1.88)	10.1	2.56 (1.58)	13.7	3.88 (3.38)	21.1
Latvia	2017	11.4	2.64 (1.74)	9.8	1.85 (1.20)	14.8	3.25 (2.72)	17.9
Lithuania	2017	15.0	2.46 (1.67)	11.2	2.16 (1.30)	18.0	3.39 (2.89)	7.7
Luxembourg	2013	11.7	2.11 (1.48)	8.6	2.24 (1.42)	14.3	3.07 (2.70)	48.3
Luxembourg	2015	9.4	2.24 (1.65)	7.1	2.25 (1.46)	11.3	3.28 (2.99)	41.2
Luxembourg	2017	8.2	2.25 (1.62)	7.3	2.10 (1.37)	11.3	3.00 (2.82)	41.8
Malta	2017	6.5	2.24 (1.86)	6.2	2.06 (1.41)	9.3	2.95 (2.99)	14.5
Netherlands	2011	7.2	1.87 (1.28)	7.2	1.75 (1.10)	10.8	2.43 (2.14)	—
Netherlands	2013	7.5	2.02 (1.54)	6.7	2.01 (1.34)	10.4	2.75 (2.60)	52.1
Netherlands	2015	6.6	2.06 (1.40)	6.0	1.67 (1.07)	9.3	2.55 (2.19)	38.2
Netherlands	2017	6.3	2.09 (1.56)	6.1	1.65 (1.10)	9.6	2.42 (2.28)	31.4
Poland	2011	17.7	2.52 (1.71)	13.6	2.27 (1.48)	21.5	3.52 (3.05)	—
Poland	2015	15.6	2.45 (1.74)	13.4	2.41 (1.55)	20.0	3.52 (3.15)	14.5
Poland	2017	13.5	2.34 (1.65)	11.2	2.25 (1.51)	17.4	3.28 (2.95)	8.2
Portugal	2011	16.8	2.36 (1.64)	12.4	1.94 (1.41)	22.0	2.90 (2.78)	—
Portugal	2015	20.8	2.50 (1.74)	13.7	2.53 (1.47)	25.1	3.45 (3.03)	16.7
Portugal	2017	21.1	2.58 (1.77)	13.0	2.60 (1.59)	24.4	3.62 (3.12)	16.6
Romania	2017	17.0	2.49 (1.72)	12.3	2.28 (1.49)	20.2	3.48 (3.00)	3.5
Slovak Republic	2017	4.7	1.72 (1.16)	4.9	1.50 (0.90)	7.6	2.05 (1.68)	14.0
Slovenia	2011	10.2	2.09 (1.41)	7.6	2.07 (1.23)	13.6	2.71 (2.37)	—
Slovenia	2013	9.4	2.30 (1.61)	8.0	2.34 (1.40)	12.9	3.14 (2.78)	15.5
Slovenia	2015	12.6	2.28 (1.59)	9.9	2.33 (1.42)	16.3	3.17 (2.81)	12.5
Slovenia	2017	10.8	2.45 (1.81)	10.2	2.64 (1.54)	15.0	3.55 (3.14)	12.1
Spain	2011	14.7	3.06 (1.91)	12.3	2.99 (1.66)	17.4	4.70 (3.62)	—
Spain	2013	12.6	2.95 (1.92)	11.6	2.92 (1.63)	15.8	4.49 (3.58)	33.9
Spain	2015	12.9	2.84 (1.87)	11.9	2.92 (1.60)	16.1	4.42 (3.47)	34.1
Spain	2017	13.8	2.95 (1.88)	13.5	2.88 (1.58)	17.5	4.55 (3.51)	31.0
Sweden	2011	11.5	2.12 (1.75)	7.9	2.62 (1.65)	14.1	3.20 (3.20)	—
Sweden	2013	8.1	2.04 (1.55)	5.8	2.14 (1.45)	10.4	2.78 (2.69)	35.8
Sweden	2015	9.5	1.78 (1.37)	6.5	1.99 (1.28)	12.1	2.46 (2.36)	30.9
Sweden	2017	9.6	2.05 (1.52)	6.9	2.02 (1.39)	12.4	2.72 (2.57)	28.9
Switzerland	2011	6.1	1.53 (1.09)	4.1	1.69 (1.11)	8.0	2.04 (1.92)	—
Switzerland	2013	5.8	1.62 (1.21)	4.0	1.60 (0.94)	7.8	2.02 (1.89)	34.0
Switzerland	2015	7.0	1.73 (1.21)	4.9	1.75 (1.15)	9.2	2.24 (2.05)	35.7

(continued)

TABLE 6A.2 Descriptive Analysis of the Prevalence and Extent of ADL/IADL Limitations and Assistance Received, Various Years, 2011–18 *(continued)*

Country	Year	ADL limitations		IADL limitations		Any ADL and IADL limitations		
		Prevalence (%)	Extent (mean (SE))	Prevalence (%)	Extent (mean (SE))	Prevalence (%)	Extent (mean (SE))	Assistance received (%)
Switzerland	2017	6.6	1.70 (1.22)	4.3	1.79 (1.17)	8.7	2.19 (2.08)	34.1
European Union	2011	12.1	2.15 (1.55)	9.7	2.08 (1.38)	15.8	2.94 (2.68)	—
European Union	2013	11.6	2.25 (1.62)	9.1	2.28 (1.45)	14.7	3.19 (2.88)	38.7
European Union	2015	11.7	2.24 (1.61)	9.4	2.24 (1.44)	14.9	3.15 (2.84)	28.7
European Union	2017	11.6	2.31 (1.66)	10.0	2.21 (1.43)	15.4	3.18 (2.88)	23.4
United Kingdom	2012	18.0	2.14 (1.47)	12.1	2.00 (1.34)	21.4	2.92 (2.52)	58.3
United Kingdom	2014	17.3	2.19 (1.48)	11.6	2.04 (1.34)	20.3	3.03 (2.54)	59.1
United Kingdom	2016	17.8	2.18 (1.51)	12.4	2.05 (1.32)	21.3	3.01 (2.56)	57.3
United Kingdom	2018	17.2	2.24 (1.53)	12.0	2.11 (1.36)	20.4	3.13 (2.64)	59.2
United States	2012	19.2	2.47 (1.67)	17.2	2.22 (1.42)	25.0	3.43 (2.90)	65.6
United States	2014	20.5	2.46 (1.65)	18.3	2.18 (1.41)	26.7	3.38 (2.86)	65.1
United States	2016	19.1	2.43 (1.61)	17.3	2.09 (1.35)	25.2	3.28 (2.78)	63.7
United States	2018	19.0	2.40 (1.60)	16.8	2.05 (1.32)	24.9	3.22 (2.68)	63.3

Source: Calculations based on data from the English Longitudinal Survey on Ageing; the Survey of Health, Ageing, and Retirement in Europe; the Health and Retirement Study; and the China Health and Retirement Longitudinal Study.
Note: ADL = activities of daily living; IADL = instrumental activities of daily living; SE = standard error; — = not available.

Notes

1. ADLs, typically learned during early childhood, are basic self-care tasks that are fundamental to independent living. Examples are walking, dressing, grooming, bathing, toileting, getting in and out of bed, and eating from a plate with utensils (Katz et al. 1963). IADLs, typically learned during adolescence, are more complex tasks that build upon the basic ADLs but require more planning and thought. Examples include driving, using public transportation, cleaning house, paying bills, managing a bank account, refilling medication prescriptions, going grocery shopping, and making a meal (Koyano et al. 1991).
2. Odds ratios for the association of older age with increased prevalence of ADL/IADL limitations range between 1.03 [95 percent confidence interval (CI): 1.02 to 1.03] in the United States and 1.11 [95 percent CI: 1.10 to 1.13] in Greece. For the association with extent of limitations, odds ratios are around 1.02.
3. Odds ratios for "with partner" range from 0.77 [95 percent CI: 0.67 to 0.90] in Greece to 1.12 [95 percent CI: 1.03 to 1.22] in France. Odds ratios for a comparison of the highest income quintile to the lowest range from 0.68 [95 percent CI: 0.62 to 0.73] in the United Kingdom to 2.01 [95 percent CI: 1.28 to 3.17] in Cyprus.

References

Anderson, Gerard, and James R. Knickman. 2001. "Changing the Chronic Care System to Meet People's Needs." *Health Affairs* 20 (6): 146–60. https://doi.org/10.1377/hlthaff.20.6.146.

Arnaert, Antonia, Bernadette Van Den Heuvel, and Tarsi Windey. 2005. "Health and Social Care Policy for the Elderly in Belgium." *Geriatric Nursing* 26 (6): 366–71. https://doi.org/10.1016/j.gerinurse.2005.09.019.

Banks, James, Michael Marmot, Zoe Oldfield, and James P. Smith. 2006. "Disease and Disadvantage in the United States and in England." *JAMA-Journal of the American Medical Association* 295 (17): 2037–45. https://doi.org/10.1001/jama.295.17.2037.

Bien, Barbara, Kevin J. McKee, Hanneli Dohner, Judith Triantafillou, Giovanni Lamura, Halina Doroszkiewicz, Barbro Krevers, and Christopher Kofahl. 2013. "Disabled Older People's Use of Health and Social Care Services and Their Unmet Care Needs in Six European Countries." *European Journal of Public Health* 23 (6): 1032–38. https://doi.org/10.1093/eurpub/cks190.

Bousquet, Guilhem, Géraldine Falgarone, David Deutsch, Sophie Derolez, Marilucy Lopez-Sublet, François-Xavier Goudot, Khadaoudj Amari, et al. 2020. "ADL-dependency, D-Dimers, LDH and Absence of Anticoagulation Are Independently Associated with One-Month Mortality in Older Inpatients with Covid-19." *Aging* 12 (12): 11306–13. https://doi.org/10.18632/aging.103583.

Case, Anne, and Angus Deaton. 2020. *Deaths of Despair and the Future of Capitalism.* Princeton, NJ: Princeton University Press.

Chen, Shanquan Q., Linda A. Jones, Shan Jiang, Huajie J. Jin, Dong Dong, Xi Chen, Dan Wang, et al. 2022. "Difficulty and Help with Activities of Daily Living among Older Adults Living Alone during the COVID-19 Pandemic: A Multi-Country Population-Based Study." *BMC Geriatrics* 22 (1): 181. https://doi.org/10.1186/s12877-022-02799-w.

Choi, HuaJung, and Robert F. Schoeni. 2017. "Health of Americans Who Must Work Longer to Reach Social Security Retirement Age." *Health Affairs* 36 (10): 1815–19. https://doi.org/10.1377/hlthaff.2017.0217.

Covinsky, Kenneth. 2006. "Aging, Arthritis, and Disability." *Arthritis & Rheumatism-Arthritis Care & Research* 55 (2): 175–76. https://doi.org/10.1002/art.21861.

Edwards, Ryan D., Willa D. Brenowitz, Elena Portacolone, Ken E. Covinsky, Andrew Bindman, M. Maria Glymour, and Jacqueline M. Torres. 2020. "Difficulty and Help with Activities of Daily Living among Older Adults Living Alone with Cognitive Impairment." *Alzheimers & Dementia* 16 (8): 1125–33. https://doi.org/10.1002/alz.12102.

Jang, Hye-Young, Young Ko, and Song-Yi Han. 2021. "The Effects of Social Networks of the Older Adults with Limited Instrumental Activities of Daily Living on Unmet Medical Needs." *International Journal of Environmental Research and Public Health* 18 (1): 27. https://doi.org/10.3390/ijerph18010027.

Katz, S., A. B. Ford, R. W. Moskowitz, B. A. Jackson, and M. W. Jaffe. 1963. "Studies of Illness in the Aged—the Index of ADL—A Standardized Measure of Biological and Psychosocial Function." *JAMA-Journal of the American Medical Association* 185 (12): 914–19. https://doi.org/10.1001/jama.1963.03060120024016.

Kiyoshige, Eri, Mai Kabayama, Yasuyuki Gondo, Yukie Masui, Hiroki Inagi, Madoka Ogawa, Takeshi Nakagawa, et al. 2019. "Age Group Differences in Association between IADL Decline and Depressive Symptoms in Community-Dwelling Elderly." *BMC Geriatrics* 19 (301): 309. https://doi.org/10.1186/s12877-019-1333-6.

Koyano, Wataru, Hioshi Shibata, Katsuharu Nakazato, Hiroshi Haga, and Yasuo Suyama. 1991. "Measurement of Competence: Reliability and Validity of the TMIG Index of

Competence." *Archives of Gerontology and Geriatrics* 13 (2): 103–16. https://doi.org /10.1016/0167-4943(91)90053-S.

Li, Mengting, and Haijing Dai. 2018. "Determining the Primary Caregiver for Disabled Older Adults in Mainland China: Spouse Priority and Living Arrangements." *Journal of Family Therapy* 41 (3): 126–41. https://doi.org/10.1111/1467-6427.12213.

Liu, H., and M. Wang. 2022. "Socioeconomic Status and ADL Disability of the Older Adults: Cumulative Health Effects, Social Outcomes and Impact Mechanisms." *PLOS One* 17 (2): e0262808.

Loyd, Christine, Alayne D. Markland, Yue Zhang, Mackenzie Fowler, Sara Harper, Nicole C. Wright, Christy S. Carter, et al. 2020. "Prevalence of Hospital-Associated Disability in Older Adults: A Meta-Analysis." *Journal of the American Medical Directors Association* 21 (4): 455–61. https://doi.org/10.1016/j.jamda.2019.09.015.

Mor, V., V. Wilcox, W. Rakowski, and J. Hiris. 1994. "Functional Transitions among the Elderly: Patterns, Predictors, and Related Hospital Use." *American Journal of Public Health* 84 (8): 1274–80. https://doi.org/10.2105/Ajph.84.8.1274.

NRC (National Research Council) Committee on National Statistics and NRC Committee on Population. 2009. *Improving the Measurement of Late-Life Disability in Population Surveys: Beyond ADLs and IADLs, Summary of a Workshop.* Washington, DC: National Academies Press. https://www.ncbi.nlm.nih.gov/books/NBK2848.

Schneider, Eric C., Arnav Shah, Michelle M. Doty, Roosa Tikkanen, Katharine Fields, and Reginald D. Williams II. 2021. *Mirror, Mirror 2021—Reflecting Poorly: Health Care in the U.S. Compared to Other High-Income Countries.* Technical Report. New York, NY: The Commonwealth Fund. doi:10.26099/01dv-h208.

Sengupta, M., L. Harris-Kojetin, J. Lendon, C. Caffrey, V. Rome, and R. Valverde. 2018. "National and State Estimates of Long-Term Care Services Users: 2016 National Study of Long-Term Care Providers." *Innovation in Aging* 2 (Suppl. 1): 474. https://doi.org/10.1093/geroni/igy023.1772.

Solé-Auró, Aïda, and Eileen M. Crimmins. 2014. "Who Cares? A Comparison of Informal and Formal Care Provision in Spain, England, and the USA." *Ageing & Society* 34 (3): 495–517. https://doi.org/10.1017/S0144686X12001134.

Steptoe, Andrew, and Giorgio Di Gessa. 2021. "Mental Health and Social Interactions of Older People with Physical Disabilities in England during the COVID-19 Pandemic: A Longitudinal Cohort Study." *Lancet Public Health* 6 (6): E365–E373. https://doi.org/10.1016/S2468-2667(21)00069-4.

WHO (World Health Organization). 2011. *World Report on Disability 2011.* Geneva: WHO. https://www.who.int/teams/noncommunicable-diseases/sensory-functions -disability-and-rehabilitation/world-report-on-disability.

CHAPTER 7

Conclusions and Policy Directions

Jigyasa Sharma, Xiaohui Hou, Feng Zhao, and Alexander Irwin

In the past four decades, nearly all countries have seen unprecedented growth in their population of older adults. This pattern is salient for high- and upper-middle-income countries, in many of which increased longevity has combined with falling fertility rates to yield rapidly aging societies. Yet populations of older people are also surging in many countries where fertility has been slower to decline and populations remain younger, on average, including some countries in South and Western Asia and most of Sub-Saharan Africa (UN DESA 2023). From 2022 to 2050, among global regions, Sub-Saharan Africa will experience by far the largest percentage increase in the number of people ages 60 and above (UN DESA 2022).

Longer life expectancy and rapidly rising numbers of older adults will transform all features of societies. To prosper in this new environment, countries will need innovative policies across many sectors. Labor markets, social protection models, health systems, the built environment, and emergency response strategies will need to evolve. The United Nations Decade of Healthy Ageing (2021–30) provides a unifying platform for the wide-ranging action that countries need to pursue, linking healthy longevity to the Sustainable Development Goals (SDGs).[1] Recent interdisciplinary research yields new evidence on the promise and challenges associated with population aging across policy domains and formulated recommendations that reflect a broad strategic vision.[2]

A Silver Opportunity to Strengthen Care Systems in Countries

The two volumes of the *Silver Opportunity* collection seek to support country action by focusing on one key component of the healthy aging agenda: person-centered, integrated care for older adults anchored in primary health care (PHC). On the one hand, this selective approach means that *Silver Opportunity* does not speak to the full range of issues that are important for older adults' well-being, many of which fall outside the health sector's direct responsibility. On the other hand, by homing in on policy and operational issues specific to older-adult care systems, *Silver Opportunity* offers know-how that decision-makers can apply to strengthen health and long-term care (LTC) services for older adults while controlling costs.

Care systems matter. Without access to quality health and social care, most older adults will not be able to realize the full promise of their longer lives and contribute all they could to their families, communities, and the economy. Without care, many will not be able to live with dignity. This work starts from the conviction that the global demographic changes now under way present a window of opportunity to assess the strengths and shortcomings of existing care systems and undertake ambitious reforms.

Today, such reforms are vital to reignite progress toward universal health coverage (UHC).[3] Encompassing access to quality essential health care services and protection against financial hardship due to health care costs, universal health care stands at the heart of the global health agenda and is integrated within the Sustainable Development Goals as SDG target 3.8. The principle of progressive universalism encourages countries to orient their UHC investments first toward those groups most at risk of poorer outcomes (Gwatkin and Ergo 2011; Rodney and Hill 2014). This principle offers a powerful argument for giving priority to PHC-centered, integrated older-adult care for countries on the path to universal health care. By restructuring care policies and programs to meet the needs of their older citizens, countries can accelerate UHC progress with equity and build healthier, more inclusive, and more prosperous societies for all.

The first volume of the *Silver Opportunity* collection (Hou, Sharma, and Zhao 2023) reviews global evidence on the need for and availability of older-adult care and makes the case for making primary health care the cornerstone of comprehensive older-adult care. It presents an original framework for country action to deliver PHC-centered, integrated health and LTC services for older adults, highlighting four action levers: financing, innovation, regulation, and evaluation (FIRE). Particularly through its case study of Japan's community-based, integrated older-adult care model (JICA, Nakayama, and Hou 2023), Volume 1 highlights the value of documenting country experiences in innovative older-adult care but also the current scarcity of country-level evidence that can readily be applied to policy.

Through four country case studies and two regional studies, *Silver Opportunity*, Volume 2, aims to narrow this evidence gap. It is not possible to draw widely generalizable policy conclusions from the *Silver Opportunity* case studies alone. However, in closing this volume, it is feasible and important to look back over all the studies and note emerging patterns that may inform policy deliberations and future research.

Taken together, the studies in this volume, linked to the prior country analyses in *Silver Opportunity*, Volume 1, yield two main types of findings. On the one hand, they bring into focus broadly consistent, high-level features of the policy environment for integrated older-adult care that influence health leaders' options across contexts. On the other hand, they capture granular policy and implementation experiences from countries under the FIRE domains. This concluding chapter summarizes these two sets of findings in turn and then discusses how countries and partners, including the World Bank, may use these results to advance older-adult care agendas in the years ahead.

Broad Features of the Policy Environment for Older-Adult Care

While each country's situation is unique, the case studies draw attention to cross-cutting factors that affect older-adult needs and policy solutions in nearly all settings. The most salient such features across our studies include the following:

- *Diversity of older-adult populations.* Older adults are not a uniform group. Within a given country, older adults differ widely in their health status and needs, socioeconomic conditions, ethnic and cultural identities, values, and goals. Sex, education, work history, rural vs. urban residence, household configuration, and exposure to varied forms of discrimination over their lifetimes mark deep differences among older adults. In Mongolia, rural elders, many of whom are nomadic, experience distinctive health risks that pose complex challenges for service delivery. The Colombia study reports that a work history in the informal versus the formal sector is associated with stark disparities in health status among the country's older adults, a pattern seen in many low- and middle-income settings (Economist Impact 2022). Worldwide, socioeconomic and health inequalities tend to accumulate and reinforce each other through the life course, meaning that health-relevant disparities may be even more pronounced for older adults than for other age groups (UN DESA 2023). Health policy and care delivery need to reflect the internal diversity of older-adult populations.

- *Growing unmet care needs.* The case studies point to large and growing gaps in PHC-centered health services and long-term care for older adults across contexts. The study of 27 European countries and 4 comparators, for example, finds substantial shortfalls in care provision for older adults with disabilities in most of the countries studied, including some of the world's wealthiest. The Sub-Saharan Africa study finds evidence of rapidly growing gaps in older-adult care across the continent, formal LTC systems in early stages of development, and traditional family care models under strain.[4] Citizens across contexts increasingly look to governments to (a) support families that want and are able to provide home-based older-adult care and (b) expand formal care systems that can offer solutions when families are not able to cope with their older members' care needs.

- *Disparate regional and country realities—with no "magic bullet."* Population aging is affecting all regions, countries, and health systems, but in different ways and at different rates. Findings from this volume's two regional studies align with broader demographic analyses (for example, UN DESA 2022, 2023). Today, among global regions, Europe and North America have the highest share of older adults in their total populations, while the individual countries with the oldest populations are in East Asia. The pace of recent population aging has been fastest in Eastern and Southeastern Asia and in Latin America and the Caribbean. But over the next three decades, Northern Africa, Western Asia, and Sub-Saharan Africa are projected to see the fastest growth in the absolute number of over-65 populations (UN DESA 2023). Against this backdrop, the 31-country study finds substantial intercountry differences in older-adult disability rates, even between countries in the same region and with similar income per capita. The diversity of regional and country experiences means that there are no uniform solutions to plan, finance, and deliver PHC-based, integrated care for older adults. Policies must reflect each country's unique health and demographic profile and development priorities. At the same time, stark differences in older-adult care needs, care receipt, and outcomes among countries with similar levels of income suggest opportunities for peer learning and performance improvement through the dissemination of effective practices.

- *Distinctive challenges and opportunities in Sub-Saharan Africa.* Patterns of demographic change in Sub-Saharan Africa are unique in important respects, as the case study confirms. The region's population remains young, on average, with nearly half of its people still under 20 years of age (UN DESA 2019). However, the absolute number of older adults is surging in many African countries, testing the region's health and social protection systems, many of which are underfunded. Spiraling burdens of noncommunicable diseases (NCDs) typically prevalent at older ages (for example, hypertension, type 2 diabetes, cardiovascular diseases) already threaten to overwhelm some African health systems (WHO AFRO 2022). The case study argues that the region's distinctive demographics highlight the policy value of "mainstreaming"—that is, integrating older-adult care priorities into broader economic and social support policies that benefit the whole population. As discussed in *Silver Opportunity*, Volume 1, strong traditions of respect for elders, family care, and community solidarity in many Sub-Saharan African societies may offer policy makers strategic advantages in advancing policy initiatives to improve older people's health and welfare (JICA, Nakayama, and Hou 2023).

- *A policy landscape in rapid evolution.* Population aging is not a "one-off" challenge. Longer lives in virtually all countries mark a structural transformation that will resonate for decades and alter every feature of societies and economies. This tectonic shift demands flexible, adaptive policy responses. Recent long-range visioning exercises such as the United States National Academy of Medicine's Global Roadmap for Healthy Longevity have sought to identify priority policy directions for the coming decade across sectors that are critical for healthy aging, while maintaining openness to the societal, technological, economic, and environmental transformations that lie ahead through mid-century but are difficult to forecast with precision (NAM 2022). Within the health sector, the best older-adult care models will show flexibility and adaptability to changing care needs at the individual, community, and country levels. This flexibility and adaptability provide support for building care solutions around community-based primary health care, arguably the care delivery modality best able to adapt to evolving local health needs while containing system costs (Bariş et al. 2021; OECD 2020).

- *Challenging but crucial action across sectors.* PHC-centered integrated health care is vital to improve health and well-being among older adults, but health care per se is just part of the picture. Advancing healthy longevity will require coordinated action across sectors, at all governance levels, and throughout the life course. By design, *Silver Opportunity* does not attempt to probe these sector-spanning issues and the relevant policy options comprehensively. However, other recent multidisciplinary research collaborations have done so (Economist Impact 2022; HLI, forthcoming; NAM 2022; O'Keefe and

Haldane 2023). Intersectoral, multisectoral, or whole-of-government action for health has long been advocated, but progress has been uneven and slow overall. Today, the evidence base on effective sector-spanning measures is growing, and some new and innovative approaches have emerged. A recent review of whole-of-society strategies to tackle noncommunicable diseases and advance healthy longevity finds limited evidence and generally insufficient evaluation of policies and programs, but also some promising initiatives, mainly, but not exclusively, in high-income and upper-middle-income countries (Govindaraj and Gopalan 2023). Models like Japan's community-based, integrated care system for older adults suggest ways that multiple governance sectors and constituencies may be engaged to deliver older-adult care attuned to local conditions and older people's preferences (JICA, Nakayama, and Hou 2023).

Policy and Implementation Experiences in the FIRE Domains

The country data and analyses presented in this volume do not aim to establish general policy norms. However, they may have illustrative value for country decision-makers trying to solve practical problems, and they suggest directions for future work. This section draws selected policy and implementation learning from the case studies, backed by the relevant analyses in *Silver Opportunity*, Volume 1. As in the prior volume, learning points are organized under the FIRE pillars: financing, innovation, regulation, and evaluation.[5] This discussion follows the case studies in considering both high-level directions for policy and more granular operational experiences that emerge from frontline programs. Both may be of interest to policy makers and system managers.

Financing

PHC investments protect vulnerable populations while fostering health system efficiency. Across global regions, countries face economic uncertainty and tightening fiscal space, reflected in the case studies and the wider literature. The costs of inpatient care continue to rise in nearly all settings, imposing heavy financial burdens on individuals, families, and national budgets (WHO and World Bank 2023). This upward trend strengthens the arguments for financing primary health care. PHC-centered care oriented to health promotion, disease prevention, and effective health system gatekeeping is the most feasible way to bend health care cost curves (Bariş et al. 2021). The case studies confirm that many countries are committed to primary health care as the mode of health care best able to meet the needs of vulnerable populations sustainably.

In addition to improving quality of care and outcomes for older adults and others, high-performing primary health care has positive spillover effects for overall health system effectiveness and efficiency (OECD 2020). The global analysis of PHC-centered care models for older adults in *Silver Opportunity*, Volume 1 (Lewis et al. 2023) highlights potential gains in care quality and cost control, while the country studies in this volume pinpoint opportunities for efficiency gains through PHC-led strategies in many of the settings studied.

The United Arab Emirates study documents substantial cost savings through the Abu Dhabi Population-at-Risk Program, thanks to a hybrid care model that reduced the number of clinic visits and hospitalizations among vulnerable older adults. In Bangladesh, the "NCD corners" integrated into some *upazila* (subdistrict) health centers show promise for efficient frontline management of chronic conditions but remain insufficiently equipped and staffed to tackle the complex multiple morbidities common in older patients. The Sub-Saharan Africa case study argues that PHC facilities in the region could be leveraged to provide basic LTC services for rapidly growing populations of older Africans at manageable cost. Relevant older-adult services might initially include chronic disease screening, health risk and disability assessments, medication management, and nursing care. This approach could help to hold down costs as countries progressively develop their LTC models, but it will only work if PHC facilities themselves are financed adequately.

Most countries have room to increase the share of their health spending invested in primary health care. The case studies also confirm that PHC systems in many countries remain underresourced, relative to the needs of aging populations, implying missed opportunities to improve efficiency and outcomes. Both Colombia and Mongolia have strong formal policy commitments to primary health care, but financing shortfalls have kept them from reaping the full benefits of a PHC-centered approach. The Bangladesh study identifies inadequate budget as a critical barrier to ensuring robust older-adult care and argues for fresh investments across the spectrum of preventive, promotive, curative, and rehabilitative activities in primary health care. Insufficient spending on PHC-led NCD prevention and care threatens health outcomes and system sustainability as Bangladesh's population ages—a pattern seen in many other countries (HLI, forthcoming; NCD Countdown 2030 Collaborators 2022). The case study recommends that Bangladesh's health sector adopt output-based budgeting to optimize yields on new investments and undertake a simultaneous cost-saving plan.

Recent analyses suggest that countries can expect to unlock large health and economic rewards by strengthening integrated care for their older-adult populations, in particular, by addressing priority noncommunicable diseases through PHC-led care across the life course (Chang et al. 2023; HLI, forthcoming; NCD Countdown 2030 Collaborators 2022). Historically, as argued in *Silver Opportunity,* Volume 1, many of today's high-income countries have grasped population aging as a political opportunity to boost public investment in health. Low- and middle-income countries in early stages of their demographic transitions have an opportunity to leverage demographic shifts in a comparable way (Fan and Savedoff 2014; Fan, Sharma, and Hou 2023).

Financing strategies for older-adult health can pursue a double objective: reduce out-of-pocket health spending and promote dignified longer lives through income support. Older adults' health outcomes and well-being are powerfully shaped by their socioeconomic conditions. Thus, some experts argue that public policy to protect older people's health must address at least two interconnected issues in the financing domain: (a) ensure older adults' access to affordable quality health care and (b) envisage income support sufficient for a dignified life in older age (Demarco et al. 2023).

Protecting individuals and households from financial hardship due to health care costs is a core thrust of universal health care, but progress in this dimension has been slow. In 2019, out-of-pocket health spending dragged 344 million people worldwide into extreme poverty and 1.3 billion into relative poverty (WHO 2023).[6] In countries where health insurance coverage and quality lag, households that include older-adult members are more likely than others to incur out-of-pocket health care costs and catastrophic health expenditures (Demarco et al. 2023). Many countries are striving to reduce out-of-pocket health care spending among the poor, older adults, and other vulnerable groups. Expanding access to health insurance is a key direction for policy. Countries like Malawi are testing innovative community-based health insurance models (Economist Impact 2022). Other strategies include abolishing or reducing user fees for health services, exempting vulnerable groups from fees, and improving care quality by nurturing providers' skills and motivation (Jalali, Bikineh, and Delavari 2021; also refer to World Bank 2019). Countries are also testing different types of income support for older people, including those who have not participated in formal labor markets. Options include, but are not limited to, noncontributory pension schemes and cash transfers (Demarco et al. 2023).

These issues surface strongly in the country and regional case studies. The Bangladesh study points to the country's current lack of adequate pension and health insurance coverage for older adults as a key barrier to realizing health gains in this population. The study authors urge the government to remedy the deficits through appropriate planning, policies, and budget allocations now. The Bangladeshi government's existing cash transfer programs, which include a focus on older women living in poverty, may provide a foundation on which to build (Economist Impact 2022).

The Colombia study likewise emphasizes income support—in particular, pensions—as a powerful lever to improve older Colombians' health and well-being, noting that this instrument has not yet been harnessed adequately. Colombia has several public and private pension schemes in place, but only 25 percent of the country's older adults are currently covered by a pension, while some 40 percent of older Colombians do not receive any public transfer or social assistance at all (Ministry of Health and Social Protection 2022). The study authors recommend urgent action to improve pension coverage for Colombia's older adults, especially those who work (or formerly worked) in the informal sector. While large unmet needs remain, Colombia's current level of pension coverage reflects meaningful progress in a relatively short time frame and gives hope for future gains in healthy aging with equity (Economist Impact 2022).

The Sub-Saharan Africa case study cites multiple policies recently adopted in African countries to provide older people with greater income security, including Mauritius' Ageing with Dignity Program and Namibia's National Pensions Act (Aboderin 2019). Some of these programs are relatively new and have not yet been robustly evaluated. However, many studies of South Africa's long-standing Old-Age Pension have linked pension receipt with substantial health gains for beneficiaries and, in some cases, health and consumption benefits for other members of the household (Lloyd-Sherlock, Agrawal, and Gómez-Olivé 2020; Ralston et al. 2015).

The Sub-Saharan Africa study finds that income support programs may enable countries to expand access to long-term care for their older citizens without committing to direct government provision of LTC services—a commitment that many countries are hesitant to adopt. Current global trends are moving away from the direct public provision of LTC services and toward private provision under government oversight (Glinskaya et al. 2023). Thus, Kenya's draft Older Persons of Society bill establishes the state's responsibility to care for people ages 60 years and older by offering a universal cash transfer for LTC services, but without specifying that the public sector must deliver the services (Aboderin 2019).

Innovation

To meet the health and other needs of growing older-adult populations while controlling costs, countries will need to develop innovative policy measures across multiple domains. The FIRE framework centers two crucial areas of innovation: (1) integrated, person-centered service delivery and (2) digital health for older adults.

Integrated Service Delivery for Older Adults

The case studies describe a range of innovative approaches to reinforce integrated service delivery for older adults. These approaches include support for family caregivers providing home-based long-term care; outreach and delivery strategies that link family-based, community-based, and professional care; targeted collaboration between the health and social welfare sectors to facilitate access to care for vulnerable older adults; and innovative measures to expand and diversify the LTC workforce.

Support for family caregivers is crucial for sustainable long-term care. The Sub-Saharan Africa study argues that, as an overarching policy goal, a mixed, balanced LTC system of informal and formal care services is desirable for African countries—an analysis that also applies in other settings (Economist Impact 2022; Glinskaya et al. 2023). Family-based care for older adults will remain the bedrock of long-term care in many regions for the foreseeable future. To achieve a balanced LTC system and sustain it over time, government support for family caregivers is needed.

Such assistance can take a variety of forms, including training and skills building, psychosocial support, referrals to community resources, and respite care (Glinskaya et al. 2023; Hinton et al. 2019). Some countries are testing direct financial support for women who provide home care to their older-adult family members (Aranco Araujo and Garcia 2023). However, others argue that this approach may reinforce gender stereotypes in caregiving and discourage women from participating in formal labor markets (Gatti et al. 2023). Country preferences will differ. For example, Chile and Uruguay have reached opposite conclusions on the issue (Aranco Araujo and Garcia 2023).

Multipronged delivery strategies can combine the strengths of family-based, community-based, and professional care. Such innovative approaches may enable countries to leverage existing grassroots care capacities, reinforcing sustainability. The Colombia case study describes the new District Care System in Bogotá, launched in 2020. The model has applied a gender lens to plan for and deliver support to older adults and their family care providers, mostly women. The District Care approach deploys three parallel outreach strategies to identify and serve vulnerable older adults and their caregivers: through mobile care units, home visits from care professionals, and grassroots care networks in local neighborhoods. The United Arab Emirates' Population-at-Risk Program also used multiple outreach and service delivery modalities in parallel to tackle health needs among vulnerable older adults during the COVID-19 pandemic. The program combined virtual medical consultations via a telehealth platform with home visits from specialized providers, home delivery of medications, and community-based testing provided by mobile units.

Collaboration between the health and social welfare sectors can expand access to key services and enhance well-being among vulnerable older adults. Growing numbers of countries are seeking innovative ways to build synergies between health and social protection agendas in the context of population aging. Japan's community-based, integrated care system is designed to harness such synergies at the local level, aligning medical and social resources in community-specific ways to meet older adults' care needs (JICA, Nakayama, and Hou 2023).

The Mongolia case study offers a concrete example from a lower-middle-income country of multisectoral collaboration in frontline primary health care. Under the mandate of a 2017 law, Mongolia's PHC facilities collaborate with the social welfare sector to deliver four key benefits of practical importance to the country's older adults, particularly those with disabilities. These benefits are (a) subsidized prices on essential medicines; (b) reimbursement for limb prostheses, orthopedic devices for hearing and vision impairments, wheelchairs, and dentures; (c) reimbursement of transport costs for older people living in remote areas who must travel to access health care; and (d) subsidization of rehabilitation costs following injury or impairment. While full-scale integration of primary health care and long-term social care remains a far-off goal in many contexts, such examples show practical advances that can be achieved more quickly and that matter for disabled and economically vulnerable older people.

Innovations in the composition and training of the health workforce can accelerate progress in older-adult care. Many of the case studies underscore health workforce challenges as key constraints affecting older-adult care systems. The Bangladesh study pinpoints human resource shortfalls as a barrier to scaling up the "NCD corner" platform for chronic disease prevention and care in subdistrict health centers. The authors also identify human resources as a limiting factor in building up Bangladesh's monitoring and evaluation (M&E) capacities for older-adult health. They recommend recruiting and training a new cadre of district-level NCD medical officers, tasked to monitor the prevalence of chronic disease and evaluate the availability and quality of frontline care for older adults.

Innovative solutions to bridge health workforce gaps are emerging in some settings. Several countries have accelerated the creation of frontline PHC delivery capacity by leveraging nontraditional workforce cadres such as community health workers. Community health workers are as good as, and sometimes better than, more formally qualified health care workers in delivering preventive, promotive, and some curative services, particularly when they are integrated with the formal health care system and work in settings that provide in-service training, financial incentives, adequate infrastructure and supplies, and regular monitoring, supervision, and evaluation (Aranco Araujo and Garcia 2023; Woldie et al. 2018).[7] The Bangladesh study argues that shifting some NCD prevention and treatment tasks from physicians to nurses and community health workers could improve the country's performance in PHC-based control of cardiovascular disease while containing costs. If effective for community-based prevention, detection, and control of cardiovascular disease, this approach could be expanded to other frontline programs.

While community health workers can contribute much, most countries also need to expand their more formally trained care workforce, enhance workers' skills, and foster employment conditions that can make paid care work more attractive to people choosing careers. The change agenda spans sectors, calls for new training pathways, and has implications for social protection and the labor force, including women's labor market participation. Investing in new cadres of health and LTC workers may help countries to advance broad human capital and job creation goals, such as boosting women's paid employment, while protecting the human capital embodied in older adults (HLI, forthcoming).

Digital Health for Older People

Digital health has the potential to transform primary health care for older populations. However, important barriers constrain progress, especially but not only in low- and middle-income countries. Obstacles commonly include lack of affordability, lack of digital skills, and shortage of user-friendly product features designed with older adults in mind (Burlac and Hou 2023). The case studies highlight digital health as a promising lever for better outcomes among elders, citing innovations that have already been achieved (in the United Arab Emirates) and analyzing future opportunities and barriers yet to be addressed (in Bangladesh and Colombia, for example). Three notable policy directions emerge.

Public-private collaboration can spur the development of digital health tools for older adults. Digital health is an area of active public-private partnerships in many countries. The United Arab Emirates case study shows that such partnerships can speed the creation and deployment of digital health tools for older people. However, robust government regulatory and oversight capacities are crucial to ensure that digital tools deliver their full promise for older adults. The authorities have worked proactively with private firms to improve digital health technologies and expand their potential applications. Proactive government oversight in the digital health space requires building appropriate staff capacities in the ministry of health and local health departments.

Observers have long noted the proliferation of digital health initiatives in Bangladesh, many driven by the country's expanding private technology sector and linked to the widespread use of mobile phones (Ahmed et al. 2014). Some of these efforts hold promise for older-adult care, especially in more remote rural areas that have been historically underserved. The Bangladesh study identifies telemedicine as a promising tool to help bridge health service delivery gaps for older adults but emphasizes the urgency of building a more robust regulatory framework and bolstering public sector monitoring capacity to ensure quality of care.

Hybrid delivery models that link telehealth with in-person care may improve uptake and satisfaction among older adults. The United Arab Emirates case study describes how Abu Dhabi's COVID-19 Population-at-Risk Program leveraged a hybrid service delivery model to improve patient uptake of services and strengthen results. The hybrid system combined telehealth with classic in-person care offered directly in patients' homes. Key to the model's success was documenting older-adult users' satisfaction with the care received. The Abu Dhabi Department of Health commissioned two large surveys of the program's beneficiary population to measure user satisfaction with several features of the service package, including the telemedicine component. Although the positive assessment rate for the telemedicine platform was high (more than 80 percent of survey respondents), users rated other aspects of the multifaceted program (for example, in-person care from doctors) even more highly, indicating additional room to support older-adult users' comfort with digital health tools and improve the tools themselves.

Age-appropriate training can boost the impacts of digital health services. The case studies confirm the importance of tailoring digital health services to older users' capacities, needs, and preferences and of not overestimating health professionals' willingness and ability to adopt these tools. The Colombia case study notes that reducing inequities in both access to and use of new information and communication technologies by older adults, especially the hearing and visually impaired, requires designing high-quality trainings for older adults in the use of these tools. Outreach and training costs need to be built into budgets from the outset, and training strategies need to be tested and iteratively improved under local conditions. The United Arab Emirates study finds impressive results for the Population-at-Risk Program overall, but reports that a large percentage of older-adult patients had difficulties with the technology used in the telemedicine component. Digital literacy among program beneficiaries ages 60 and older was generally low. The authors conclude that patient education is critical for the success and sustainability of such programs.

Regulation and Governance

Regulatory tools are among governments' most powerful instruments to improve older people's health and secure their access to quality services. As the need for old-age care expands across global regions and traditional family-based care solutions come under stress, comprehensive regulation and oversight of older-adult care emerge as a salient responsibility for governments in all countries.

Equitable access to quality care for older adults will not happen automatically, no matter how high a country's income. Deliberate government action is always required. Key directions for this effort emerge from the case studies: anchoring regulation in a commitment to older people's dignity, ensuring a comprehensive legal and regulatory framework for all modes of older-adult care, building implementation capacity in step with regulatory reforms, and "mainstreaming" older-adult care and support into policies that benefit the whole population.

The cornerstone of regulation is the dignity of older people. While governance in older-adult care poses many challenges, it has a clear guiding principle: ensuring older adults' dignity. Ensuring dignity involves systematically engaging older people, their families, and communities as active partners in clarifying their care needs and preferences, setting policy goals, defining implementation strategies, and monitoring results. Some countries have achieved notable success in creating governance approaches that protect and enhance older people's dignity. The community-based, integrated care model in Japan and recent community LTC initiatives in Thailand offer examples (Kondo, Sato, and Nagamine 2023). The philosophies and engagement strategies that inform these models may be adapted to other settings. Key is an inclusive vision that both embraces and looks beyond health care per se to recognize the full range of grassroots care capabilities and relevant social resources present in communities (JICA, Nakayama, and Hou 2023).

The Colombia case study describes a model taking a holistic, locally grounded approach to service delivery designed to foster "aging in place" with dignity. In particular, the District Care model recognizes gendered asymmetries in older-adult care needs, care access, and delivery roles that are likely to affect dignity differently for women and men. The Mongolia study recommends an ambitious national strategy for older-adult health and well-being, encompassing improvements in PHC-led clinical care but also a commitment to address other prerequisites for aging with dignity, such as confronting ageism in society and expanding access to long-term care.

Active participation by older adults in the policy choices that affect them is essential to ensure their dignity and rights. Recent research has clarified both (a) the political rationale for expanding public participation in decision-making around health goals and (b) specific modalities that countries can use to facilitate participation (World Bank, NIPH, and BCEPS 2023). The research identifies practical engagement tools that cover a spectrum from lower to higher resource intensity. Examples range from "light-touch" data-gathering and opinion-gathering instruments like surveys to more ambitious (and costlier) participatory mechanisms like citizens' juries or consultative panels. Examples of the latter include the multistakeholder panels that Thai health authorities regularly convene to advise on updates to the country's universal health coverage scheme (Kantamaturapoj et al. 2020).

As discussed in *Silver Opportunity*, Volume 1, such approaches to inclusive policy making can be complemented by service delivery models in which older adults and their grassroots organizations function as care providers. These delivery models affirm older people's agency while leveraging their distinctive know-how and networks to foster self-care and mutual care within the community (JICA, Nakayama, and Hou 2023). Local older people's organizations have launched participatory service delivery models in several Asian countries, including Bangladesh, Cambodia, India, Nepal, the Philippines, and Viet Nam (Economist Impact 2022; Hou et al. 2023).

An adequate legal and regulatory framework encompasses all aspects of older-adult care and defines clear roles for government and private actors. Regulation is especially important in areas that are evolving rapidly under the impact of market forces, including digital health and long-term care. Public-private collaboration in these domains brings potential for innovation and efficiency gains but also conflicts of interest, poor-quality services, abuse, and neglect, with grave consequences for vulnerable older adults (Glinskaya et al. 2023). Governance tools to boost quality include both incentives that can motivate private actors to improve care voluntarily and binding regulations that can force them to do so. Preferences for "carrots" versus "sticks" will reflect a country's political economy, administrative organization, and the development phase of local care systems (Kondo, Sato, and Nagamine 2023).

Historically, regulatory oversight of long-term care has been a low policy priority in most low- and middle-income countries (Glinskaya et al. 2023). The Mongolia case identifies an array of laws that govern health care provision, including for older adults. However, LTC regulation in the country is in early stages. Such patterns may change as countries expand their public financing of LTC services. When governments acquire a greater financial stake in LTC systems—for example, by building public reimbursement mechanisms that help individuals and families to pay for long-term care—they may be better positioned to demand regulatory compliance and quality assurance from private providers (Feng 2019). For this reason, all countries, even those whose populations are still relatively young, have an interest in developing comprehensive, long-range plans for public sector–led LTC financing, ideally working toward a broad-based, universal-coverage social insurance model like the models adopted in Germany, Japan, and the Republic of Korea (Feng et al. 2020; Glinskaya et al. 2023).

Countries need to build implementation capacity in step with regulatory reforms and service guarantees. While strong legal and regulatory frameworks are essential to support healthy aging, they are only a first step. Several of the case studies underline the importance for countries of closing the gaps between regulations, rights, and service guarantees that exist on paper and the realization of entitlements through effective care provision, including enforcement capacity when abuses are detected or service quality falls short. This need applies to health care service packages, LTC models, and other key features of comprehensive care for older adults.

The Bangladesh study notes that, in 2013, the country adopted a policy formally establishing the state's responsibility to secure the basic rights of older Bangladeshis, including their access to affordable quality health care. However, the financial and technical means to operationalize these legal entitlements have not been mobilized. No practical strategy or costed action plan related to older-adult health has yet been put forward in Bangladesh. In practice, the country's older adults must still commonly contend with shortfalls in both core dimensions of universal health care: access to essential services and financial protection. In Colombia, older adults are also guaranteed universal access to affordable quality health care in principle, but implementation capacity lags. In some parts of the country, local governments have introduced promising strategies. In the mostly agricultural district of Sumapaz, the local government's funding of the Comprehensive Care Model for Rural Health through two decades has improved access to high-quality health care, benefiting older adults in rural communities (Economist Impact 2022).

Some governments are choosing to "mainstream" older-adult care and support, integrating these objectives into agendas that benefit the whole population. As highlighted in the Sub-Saharan Africa case study, the African Union (AU) Policy Framework and Plan of Action on Ageing encourages countries to mainstream their older-adult care policies in this way (Aboderin 2008). This mainstreaming can be achieved by integrating policies that support healthy aging across all adult age groups into larger plans related to socioeconomic development, rather than targeting older persons as a distinct group for special earmarked services. Following the establishment of the AU Plan, several African countries have developed new policies for older-adult care and support, some of which reflect a mainstreaming approach. Such strategies may offer important political advantages. They preempt the risk of casting older adults as a privileged constituency whose needs are given disproportionate attention, a perception that has fueled intergenerational tensions in some settings (Scott 2021).

Beyond the political optics of dedicated investments in older-adult care, there are sound public health and economic arguments for mainstreaming. People's health status as older adults largely reflects their health earlier in life (HLI, forthcoming). Thus, optimizing health and human capital in older people requires a life-course approach, featuring robust health promotion and NCD prevention and control at all ages (O'Keefe and Haldane 2023). Integrated PHC systems able to deliver quality care to older people also generally serve other population groups well (Lewis et al. 2023). Arguably, investments in strong community-based primary health care thus provide an automatic form of mainstreaming, improving outcomes for older adults while benefiting the broader population. This reciprocity underpins the link between PHC-centered integrated older-adult care and UHC goals analyzed in *Silver Opportunity*, Volume 1.

Evaluation and Measurement

Evaluation and measurement are key to understanding older people's care needs and ensuring that the supply of services matches the demand. In a context of tight government budgets and multiple health challenges, rigorous evaluation becomes even more important to ensure that scarce health system resources are used to best effect. The case studies confirm previous research reporting major gaps in country-level data and evaluation of older-adult care needs and care provision. However, the case studies also capture strategies that have begun to narrow the gaps in monitoring and evaluation in some countries.

Foundational steps in evaluation include harmonizing data tools across partner agencies and disaggregating key health data for older adults. Authors of the Bangladesh case study note that the country has in place some mechanisms for collecting digital health data—for example, on priority noncommunicable diseases—but the data are currently not disaggregated for seniors and nonseniors. NCD data are collected and managed as per the national protocol under Bangladesh's program for hypertension and diabetes control, for example, but different development partners are supporting the activities with different, incompatible types of software. This incompatibility leads to fragmentation and limits the potential for data sharing and comprehensive analysis across platforms, essential to track trends and adequately evaluate the impact of policies and programs.

Recent work linked to the Disease Control Priorities project has shown how countries working toward universal health coverage may strengthen and harmonize monitoring and evaluation of their essential health services package in ways that reinforce local M&E skills and strengthen national health information systems (Danforth et al. 2023). For example, countries may achieve best M&E results by using a combination of core indicators derived from global frameworks (for example, the UHC indicators defined for SDGs 3.8.1 and 3.8.2) and country-specific indicators linked to the national essential health services package and local needs. To the fullest extent possible, data collection should be integrated into routine frontline service provision activities with existing staff. And M&E work should be driven and owned by the national ministry of health rather than development partners or consultants (Danforth et al. 2023).

As they pursue these agendas, countries and their development partners can choose to adopt open-data models within national statistical systems and across partner agencies, helping to make open data the "new normal" for twenty-first-century development. Doing so will facilitate knowledge sharing and partnerships across countries. Peer-to-peer learning and network building for better evaluation will strengthen health system capacities in critical areas, including older-adult health but also frontline primary health care more broadly and pandemic preparedness (HLI, forthcoming; World Bank 2022).

Strong, well-planned evaluation is vital to demonstrate the health impacts and cost savings that may be generated by innovative care programs for older adults, convincing decision-makers of the value of these investments. Building in robust evaluation from the start is key to effective program design and budgeting. The United Arab Emirates case study provides an example of how smart monitoring and evaluation can quantify the benefits of innovative interventions, helping to make the case for further investment. The managers of the Abu Dhabi Population-at-Risk Program ensured rigorous tracking of process and outcome measures to document program performance and the value for money obtained. Monitoring showed that in diabetes care, for example, of 593 patients who provided their glycated hemoglobin A1c results before and after enrolling with one of the program's four provider organizations, more than 45 percent improved their diabetes management. Leveraging other monitoring data, program leaders were able to show that the hybrid Population-at-Risk service model, with its telehealth and home-support components, had prevented more than 10,000 unnecessary hospital or clinic visits and admissions in the first quarter of 2022 alone, generating substantial cost savings. Documentation of such results likely played a role in convincing Department of Health officials to develop and expand the groundbreaking program beyond the COVID-19 emergency.

Appropriately defining the goals set in M&E frameworks may help to improve the results obtained from activities such as population-based health screening. The authors of the Mongolia case study note that the country's government recognizes the importance of providing population-based screening to improve health outcomes and reduce mortality rates. To date, however, the M&E frameworks established for these important programs have been aligned to overly broad health goals—for example, raising life expectancy, reducing gaps in life expectancy, or decreasing the incidence of cancer. Such sweeping, high-level health goals are clearly important, but they are associated with many factors beyond early detection of priority diseases. Thus, evaluating screening programs against these indicators may yield misleading results. The authors propose a more specific definition of goals and outcomes for monitoring—for example, increasing the percentage of cases diagnosed at earlier stages, increasing survival rates, or reducing the costs per detected case. Adopting more practical indicators may improve performance in population-based screening, boost the motivation of care providers and managers, and ultimately facilitate population health gains.

To strengthen evaluation of older-adult care and outcomes, countries can leverage multipartner, collaborative platforms such as national observatories. The Colombia case study calls for action to bolster the institutional capacities necessary to deliver the country's National Public Policy on Aging and Old Age 2022–2031. For the study authors, strengthening monitoring and evaluation is a high priority. They argue that this agenda can be advanced by reinforcing Colombia's recently launched National Observatory on Aging and Old Age, in coordination with other observatories in the country that gather, analyze, and publish key health and social data relevant to the well-being of older adults.

The concept of an observatory for monitoring trends in health and society arose in the 1960s by analogy with astronomical facilities and from the realization that consistent observation is essential to understand dynamics in any community (Guidotti 2022; Hackenberg 1967). In Europe, observatories tracking many aspects of population health have been introduced at national, regional, and local levels (Guidotti 2022). The observatory model has gained broad application in Latin America in health and other public policy domains (OAS 2015).[8]

Depending on where observatories are anchored institutionally and the number and types of partners involved, they may have a public, private, or mixed public-private character. From a policy standpoint, their purpose is to serve as information systems that produce, systematize, and disseminate knowledge in specified areas of importance for governance (OAS 2015). This role often involves longitudinal data collection but may encompass a range of other analytic, evaluative, advisory, and knowledge-sharing functions (Guidotti 2022). Colombia's experience suggests that countries working to enhance health service delivery and outcomes among older adults may benefit from creating or upgrading national observatories that can link the strengths of the public administration, academic research, and civil society to track policy implementation, assess results, and capture lessons for continued improvement.

Summary of Policy and Implementation Takeaways

Evidence of effective measures to strengthen older-adult care systems remains limited, especially for low- and middle-income countries. The *Silver Opportunity* case studies aim to narrow this knowledge gap and support informed policy making in countries going forward. Table 7.1 organizes the main policy and delivery findings from the case studies discussed in this chapter.

The results summarized here are one step in learning about how countries can deliver integrated, PHC-centered care for older adults. They are not the end of the journey. The takeaways derived from these country experiences must be debated, tested, adapted, and improved in future work.

A broad horizon for research—including operational research in service delivery—is opening as countries gear up to expand their provision of integrated, PHC-led services for older adults, particularly targeting noncommunicable diseases (Alleyne et al. 2023; Jamison et al. 2017; NCD Countdown 2030 Collaborators 2022). The case studies provide data that can inform future analyses on topics that have been touched on in the *Silver Opportunity* research but where important questions remain open. These questions include optimal prioritization and sequencing of older-adult care interventions in primary health care, the integration of primary health care and long-term care, and effective multisectoral strategies (Jamison et al. 2017; OECD 2017).

TABLE 7.1 Policy and Implementation Takeaways from the *Silver Opportunity* Case Studies

FIRE domain	Takeaways
Financing	• PHC investments protect vulnerable populations while fostering health system efficiency. • Most countries have room to increase the share of their health spending invested in PHC. • Some countries are crafting investments in older-adult health to reduce out-of-pocket health spending and promote dignified lives through income support.
Innovation (care delivery)	• Support for family caregivers is crucial for sustainable LTC. Options include training and skills building, psychosocial support, and referral to community resources. • Promising multipronged service delivery strategies link family-based, community-based, and professional care for older adults. • Targeted collaboration between the health and social welfare sectors can improve care access and enhance well-being for vulnerable older people. • Health workforce innovations like the deployment of community health workers can expand care coverage while containing costs.
Innovation (digital health)	• Public-private collaboration can spur the development of age-friendly digital health tools. • Hybrid delivery models that link telehealth with in-person care may improve service uptake and outcomes for older adults. • Training care providers and older-adult users can improve the uptake and impact of digital health tools.
Regulation and governance	• The cornerstone of effective regulation is the dignity of older people. • An adequate legal and regulatory framework encompasses all aspects of older-adult care. Currently, LTC regulation lags in many countries. • Countries need to build implementation capacity in step with regulatory reforms and service guarantees. • "Mainstreaming" integrates older-adult care and support into policies that benefit the whole population.
Evaluation and measurement	• Foundational steps in M&E for older-adult health include harmonizing data tools across partner agencies and disaggregating data. • Documenting health impacts and cost savings linked to innovative older-adult programs can strengthen the case for more investment. • Appropriately defining program goals in M&E frameworks may improve population-based health screening. • To strengthen measurement in older-adult care, countries can leverage flexible collaborative platforms such as national observatories.

Source: Compilation of findings from the *Silver Opportunity* case studies.
Note: FIRE = financing, innovation, regulation, and evaluation; LTC = long-term care; M&E = monitoring and evaluation; PHC = primary health care.

The Way Forward: Strengthening Older-Adult Care on the Path to Universal Health Care

Longer lives in all countries reflect historic development achievements and pave the way for future gains. In 2015, all United Nations member states embraced a comprehensive development agenda under the SDGs. The goals include ambitious targets in poverty reduction, gender equality, education, health, clean energy, and other domains. Countries have pledged to achieve these targets, including universal health coverage, by 2030, recognizing healthy aging as integral to success.[9]

Today, at the midpoint of the SDG timeline, many of the goals are at risk (UN 2023). Performance on UHC indicators has lagged in most countries (WHO 2023). As health leaders work to reignite momentum for universal health care, *Silver Opportunity* has made the case that strengthening PHC-centered integrated care for older adults can accelerate UHC progress.

Primary responsibility for crafting and implementing older-adult care models rests with governments. Equitable healthy aging is achievable—even in societies with large informal economies and limited institutional capacity—but requires sustained political commitment (Economist Impact 2022). Supporting government action, other stakeholders can contribute powerfully to the work. These stakeholders include institutional development partners, the private sector, academic researchers, and civil society actors at global, national, and local levels, especially organizations of older people and their advocates.

United Nations and World Health Organization leadership on healthy aging has opened paths for progress during the Decade of Healthy Ageing (2021–30) and beyond—for example, by documenting critical evidence gaps and strengthening monitoring systems for healthy aging (WHO 2020); developing normative tools and guidelines for older-adult care, including health services and long-term care (WHO 2021); amplifying older adults' voices in international forums; and combating ageist discrimination in its many forms worldwide, including within health systems (WHO 2015, 2020). Other technical and development agencies, including the World Bank, can leverage their specific capabilities to back country action for achieving healthier longer lives.

The World Bank supports countries in managing the complex challenges and opportunities associated with population aging. The World Bank's added value in this area reflects the organization's capacity to combine flexible development financing with policy and implementation support across sectors that include health, social protection and jobs, climate and energy, transport, public financial management, and others.

The *Silver Opportunity* work on integrated older-adult care systems is one facet of this agenda. It responds to rising demand from countries and builds on the World Bank's experience in supporting strategic health system reform in partnership with other development actors and global technical agencies, notably the World Health Organization. Support for countries that want to organize older-adult care services around primary health care leverages and reinforces these collaborations. It reflects the far-reaching demographic and epidemiological changes now under way in countries and the lessons learned from recent crises, including COVID-19 (World Bank 2022). The work seeks to enable countries to meet current health challenges while ensuring that their health systems are resilient and future-fit.

By building PHC-centered, integrated older-adult care systems, countries can advance health and development for their whole populations. The obstacles to achieving these aims are formidable. The country policy and implementation strategies described in these pages represent modest but meaningful steps forward. As they adapt existing evidence-based solutions, improve them through fresh innovations, and share results, countries will grasp silver opportunities for older people and for all.

Notes

1. For information on the Decade of Healthy Ageing, refer to https://www .decadeofhealthyageing.org.
2. Key recent interdisciplinary research and policy contributions in this space include the Aging Readiness and Competitiveness reports from Economist Impact and the American Association of Retired Persons (for example, Economist Impact 2022); the Global Healthy Longevity Road Map from the United States Academy of Medicine (NAM 2022); the technical papers and synthesis report from the World Bank Healthy Longevity Initiative (HLI, forthcoming); and the World Health Organization's work on aging and health over more than a decade (for example, WHO 2015, 2020, 2021).
3. For details, refer to https://www.who.int/news-room/fact-sheets/detail/universal -health-coverage-(uhc).
4. These results align with the findings of previous analyses, including those presented in *Silver Opportunity*, Volume 1, and recent work for the Healthy Longevity Initiative on LTC needs and service provision in low- and middle-income countries (Glinskaya et al. 2023).
5. The issues highlighted here do not exhaust the policy- and practice-relevant learning that the case studies contain. Readers are encouraged to explore the core chapters of this volume and consult the longer background studies and supplementary data, which are available at https://documents.worldbank.org/en/publication/documents -reports/documentlist?colti=%22silver%20opportunity%20case%20study%20 series%22&srt=docdt&order=desc. The following pages emphasize select country and regional findings that align with and enrich the policy takeaways presented in the concluding chapter of *Silver Opportunity*, Volume 1.
6. Refer to https://www.who.int/news-room/fact-sheets/detail/universal-health -coverage-(uhc).
7. Of note, community health workers played a key role in some of the most effective country-level responses to the early phases of the COVID-19 pandemic by strengthening frontline prevention, case detection, and care. Thailand offers one example (Haldane et al. 2021).
8. Regional and global institutions including the European University Institute; the United Nations Educational, Scientific, and Cultural Organization; and the World Bank have also adopted the observatory model to guide programs in economic and social development (Guidotti 2022).
9. Refer to https://www.who.int/initiatives/decade-of-healthy-ageing#:~:text=The%20 United%20Nations%20Decade%20of,communities%20in%20which%20they%20 live.

References

Aboderin, Isabella. 2008. "Linking Ageing to Development Agendas in Sub-Saharan Africa: Challenges and Approaches." *Journal of Population Ageing* 1 (1): 51–73. https:// doi.org/10.1007/s12062-009-9002-8.

Aboderin, Isabella. 2019. "Toward a Fit-for-Purpose Policy Architecture on Long-Term Care in Sub-Saharan Africa: Impasse and a Research Agenda to Overcome It." *Journal of Long-Term Care* (September 13, 2019): 119–26. https://doi.org/10.31389/jltc.5.

Ahmed, Tanvir, Henry Lucas, Azfar S. Khan, Rubana Islam, Abbas Bhuiya, and Mohammad Iqbal. 2014. "eHealth and mHealth Initiatives in Bangladesh: A Scoping Study." *BMC Health Services Research* 14 (260). https://doi.org/10.1186/1472-6963-14-260.

Alleyne, George, Timothy Evans, Alec Irwin, Prabhat Jha, and Jeremy Veillard. 2023. "Enhancing Human Capital and Boosting Productivity by Tackling Non-Communicable Diseases: Results of a Research Initiative." Background paper for the World Bank Healthy Longevity Initiative, World Bank, Washington, DC.

Aranco Araujo, Natalia, and Gisela M. Garcia. 2023. "Health and Long-Term Care Needs in a Context of Rapid Population Aging." Background study for the World Bank Healthy Longevity Initiative, World Bank, Washington, DC.

Barış, Enis, Rachel Silverman, Huijui Wang, Feng Zhao, and Muhammad Ali Pate. 2021. *Walking the Talk: Reimagining Primary Health Care after COVID-19.* Washington, DC: World Bank. https://openknowledge.worldbank.org/handle/10986/35842.

Burlac, Gabriel, and Xiaohui Hou. 2023. "How Digital Health Technology Is Transforming Health Care for Older Adults." In *Silver Opportunity: Building Integrated Services for Older Adults around Primary Health Care,* edited by Xiaohui Hou, Jigyasa Sharma, and Feng Zhao. Washington, DC: World Bank.

Chang, Angela Y., Gretchen A. Stevens, Diego S. Cardoso, Bochen Cao, and Dean T. Jamison. 2023. "The Economic Burden of Disease—Monetizing the Benefits of Preventing Avoidable Mortality." Background study for the World Bank Healthy Longevity Initiative, World Bank, Washington, DC.

Danforth, Kristen, Ahsan M. Ahmad, Karl Blanchet, Muhammad Khalid, Arianna R. Means, Solomon T. Memirie, Ala Alwan, and David Watkins. 2023. "Monitoring and Evaluating the Implementation of Essential Packages of Health Services." *BMJ Global Health* 8 (Suppl. 1): e010726. https://doi.org/10.1136/bmjgh-2022-010726.

Demarco, Gustavo, Johannes Koettl, Miglena Abels, and Andrea Petrelli. 2023. "Adequacy of Pensions and Access to Health Care: Maintaining Human Capital during Old Age." Background study for the World Bank Healthy Longevity Initiative, World Bank, Washington, DC.

Economist Impact. 2022. *Achieving Equitable Healthy Aging in Low- and Middle-Income Countries: The Aging Readiness & Competitiveness Report 4.0.* Washington, DC: AARP International.

Fan, Victoria Y., and William D. Savedoff. 2014. "The Health Financing Transition: A Conceptual Framework and Empirical Evidence." *Social Science and Medicine* 105 (March): 112–21.

Fan, Victoria Y., Jigyasa Sharma, and Xiaohui Hou. 2023. "Financing Primary Health Care for Older Adults: Framework and Applications." In *Silver Opportunity: Building Integrated Services for Older Adults around Primary Health Care,* edited by Xiaohui Hou, Jigyasa Sharma, and Feng Zhao. Washington, DC: World Bank.

Feng, Zhanlian. 2019. "Global Convergence: Aging and Long-Term Care Policy Challenges in the Developing World." *Journal of Aging and Social Policy* 31 (4): 291–97. https://doi.org/10.1080/08959420.2019.1626205.

Feng, Zhanlian, Elena Glinskaya, Hongtu Chen, Sen Gong, Yue Qiu, Jianming Xu, and Winnie Yip. 2020. "Long-Term Care System for Older Adults in China: Policy Landscape, Challenges, and Future Prospects." *The Lancet* 396 (10259): 1362–72. https://doi.org/10.1016/S0140-6736(20)32136-X.

Gatti, Roberta, Daniel Halim, Allen Hardiman, and Shuqiao Sun. 2023. "Gendered Responsibilities, Elderly Care, and Labor Supply: Evidence from Four Middle-Income Countries." Background study for the World Bank Healthy Longevity Initiative, World Bank, Washington, DC.

Glinskaya, Elena, Xiaohui Hou, Zhanlian Feng, Guadalupe Suarez, Jigyasa Sharma, Drystan Phillips, Jenny Wilkens, et al. 2023. "Demand for and Supply of Long-Term Care for Older Persons in Low- and Middle-Income Countries." Background study for the World Bank Healthy Longevity Initiative, World Bank, Washington, DC.

Govindaraj, Ramesh, and Sundararajan Srinivasa Gopalan. 2023. "Control of Non-Communicable Diseases for Enhanced Human Capital: The Case for Whole-of-Society Action." Background study for the World Bank Healthy Longevity Initiative, World Bank, Washington, DC.

Guidotti, Tee L. 2022. "The Observatory: A Model for Studies in Health, Society, and the Environment." *Journal of Environmental Studies and Sciences* 12 (4): 827–37. https://doi.org/10.1007/s13412-022-00786-6.

Gwatkin, Davidson R., and Alex Ergo. 2011. "Universal Health Coverage: Friend or Foe of Health Equity?" *The Lancet* 377 (9784): 2160–61. https://doi.org/10.1016/S0140-6736(10)62058-2.

Hackenberg, Robert A. 1967. "The Social Observatory: Time Series Data for Health and Behavioral Research." *Social Science and Medicine (1970)* 4 (3): 343–57.

Haldane, Victoria, Chuan De Foo, Salma M. Abdalla, Anne Sophie Jung, Melisa Tan, Shishi Wu, Alvin Chua, et al. 2021. "Health Systems Resilience in Managing the COVID-19 Pandemic: Lessons from 28 Countries." *Nature Medicine* 27 (6): 964–80. https://doi.org/10.1038/s41591-021-01381-y.

Hinton, Ladson, Duyen Tran, Thuc-Nhi Nguyen, Janis Ho, and Laura Gitlin. 2019. "Interventions to Support Family Caregivers of People Living with Dementia in High, Middle, and Low-Income Countries in Asia: A Scoping Review." *BMJ Global Health* 4 (6): e001830.

HLI (Healthy Longevity Initiative). Forthcoming. *Unlocking the Power of Healthy Longevity: Tackling Non-Communicable Diseases to Save Lives, Improve Wellbeing, Reduce Inequities, and Strengthen Human Capital.* Washington, DC: World Bank.

Hou, Xiaohui, Jigyasa Sharma, and Feng Zhao, eds. 2023. *Silver Opportunity: Building Integrated Services for Older Adults around Primary Health Care.* Washington, DC: World Bank.

Hou, Xiaohui, Jigyasa Sharma, Feng Zhao, and Alexander Irwin. 2023. "Conclusions and Policy Takeaways." In *Silver Opportunity: Building Integrated Services for Older Adults around Primary Health Care,* edited by Xiaohui Hou, Jigyasa Sharma, and Feng Zhao. Washington, DC: World Bank.

Jalali, Faride S., Parisa Bikineh, and Sajad Delavari. 2021. "Strategies for Reducing Out of Pocket Payments in the Health System: A Scoping Review." *Cost Effectiveness and Resource Allocation* 19 (1): 47. https://doi.org/10.1186/s12962-021-00301-8.

Jamison, Dean T., Helen Gelband, Susan Horton, Prabhat Jha, Ramanan Laxminarayan, Charles N. Mock, and Rachel Nugent, eds. 2017. *Disease Control Priorities: Improving Health and Reducing Poverty. Disease Control Priorities,* 3d ed., vol. 9. Washington, DC: World Bank.

JICA (Japan International Cooperation Agency), Risa Nakayama, and Xiaohui Hou. 2023. "Community-Based Integrated Care in Japan." In *Silver Opportunity: Building Integrated Services for Older Adults around Primary Health Care,* edited by Xiaohui Hou, Jigyasa Sharma, and Feng Zhao. Washington, DC: World Bank.

Kantamaturapoj, Kanang, Anond Kulthanmanusorn, Woranan Witthayapipopsakul, Shaheda Viriyathorn, Walaiporn Patcharanarumol, Churnrurtai Kanchanachitra, Suwit Wibulpolprasert, and Viroj Tangcharoensathien. 2020. "Legislating for Public Accountability in Universal Health Coverage, Thailand." *Bulletin of the World Health Organization* 98 (2): 117–25. https://dx.doi.org/10.2471/BLT.19.239335.

Kondo, Naoki, Koryu Sato, and Yuiko Nagamine. 2023. "Designing Integrated Care for an Aging Population: Regulation and Governance for Healthy Aging." In *Silver Opportunity: Building Integrated Services for Older Adults around Primary Health Care,* edited by Xiaohui Hou, Jigyasa Sharma, and Feng Zhao. Washington, DC: World Bank.

Lewis, Todd P., Margaret E. Kruk, Jigyasa Sharma, and Xiaohui Hou. 2023. "High-Quality Health Systems for an Aging Population: Primary Care Models with Users at the Center." In *Silver Opportunity: Building Integrated Services for Older Adults around Primary Health Care,* edited by Xiaohui Hou, Jigyasa Sharma, and Feng Zhao. Washington, DC: World Bank.

Lloyd-Sherlock, Peter, Sutapa Agrawal, and Francesc Xavier Gómez-Olivé. 2020. "Pensions, Consumption, and Health: Evidence from Rural South Africa." *BMC Public Health* 20 (1): 1577. https://doi.org/10.1186/s12889-020-09666-6.

Ministry of Health and Social Protection. 2022. "Resolución 1035 de 2022." Ministry of Health and Social Protection, Bogotá.

NAM (United States National Academy of Medicine). 2022. *Global Roadmap for Healthy Longevity.* Washington, DC: National Academies Press. https://doi.org/10.17226/26144.

NCD Countdown 2030 Collaborators. 2022. "NCD Countdown 2030: Efficient Pathways and Strategic Investments to Accelerate Progress towards the Sustainable Development Goal Target 3.4 in Low-Income and Middle-Income Countries." *The Lancet* 399 (10331): 1266–78.

OAS (Organization of American States). 2015. *Public Policy Observatories in the Americas: A Guide for Their Design and Implementation in Our Public Administrations.* Washington, DC: OAS.

OECD (Organisation for Economic Co-operation and Development). 2017. *Preventing Ageing Unequally.* Paris: OECD Publishing. https://doi.org/10.1787/9789264279087-en.

OECD (Organisation for Economic Co-operation and Development). 2020. *Realising the Potential of Primary Health Care.* OECD Health Policy Studies. Paris: OECD.

O'Keefe, Philip, and Victoria Haldane. 2023. "Towards a Framework for Impact Pathways between NCDs, Human Capital, and Healthy Longevity: Economic and Wellbeing Outcomes." Background study for the World Bank Healthy Longevity Initiative, World Bank, Washington, DC.

Ralston, Margaret, Enid Schatz, Jane Menken, Francesc Xavier Gómez-Olivé, and Stephen Tollman. 2015. "Who Benefits—Or Does Not—From South Africa's Old Age Pension? Evidence from Characteristics of Rural Pensioners and Non-Pensioners." *International Journal of Environmental Research and Public Health* 13 (1): 85. https://doi.org/10.3390/ijerph13010085.

Rodney, Anna M., and Peter S. Hill. 2014. "Achieving Equity within Universal Health Coverage: A Narrative Review of Progress and Resources for Measuring Success." *International Journal for Equity in Health* 13: Art. 72. https://doi.org/10.1186/s12939-014-0072-8.

Scott, Andrew J. 2021. "The Longevity Economy." *The Lancet Healthy Longevity* 2 (12): e828–e835.

UN (United Nations). 2023. *The Sustainable Development Goals Report 2023. Special Edition.* New York: United Nations.

UN DESA (United Nations Department of Economic and Social Affairs). 2019. *World Population Prospects 2019: Highlights.* ST/ESA/SER.A/423. New York: UN DESA, Population Division.

UN DESA (United Nations Department of Economic and Social Affairs). 2022. *World Population Prospects 2022* (online edition). New York: UN DESA, Population Division. https://population.un.org/wpp.

UN DESA (United Nations Department of Economic and Social Affairs). 2023. *World Social Report 2023: Leaving No One Behind in an Ageing World.* New York: UN DESA.

WHO (World Health Organization). 2015. *World Report on Aging and Health.* Geneva: WHO. https://apps.who.int/iris/handle/10665/186/463.

WHO (World Health Organization). 2020. *Decade of Healthy Ageing Baseline Report.* Geneva: WHO.

WHO (World Health Organization). 2021. *Framework for Countries to Achieve an Integrated Continuum of Long-Term Care*. Geneva: WHO.

WHO (World Health Organization). 2023. "Universal Health Coverage: Key Facts." Online fact sheet. WHO, Geneva. https://www.who.int/news-room/fact-sheets /detail/universal-health-coverage-(uhc).

WHO AFRO (World Health Organization Regional Office for Africa). 2022. *Tracking Universal Health Coverage in the WHO African Region, 2022*. Brazzaville: WHO Regional Office for Africa.

WHO (World Health Organization) and World Bank. 2023. *Tracking Universal Health Coverage: 2023 Global Monitoring Report: Executive Summary*. Geneva: World Health Organization; Washington, DC: World Bank.

Woldie, Mirkuzie, Garumma Tolu Feyissa, Bitiya Admasu, Kalkidan Hassen, Kirstin Mitchell, Susannah Mayhew, Martin McKee, and Dina Balabanova. 2018. "Community Health Volunteers Could Help Improve Access to and Use of Essential Health Services by Communities in LMICs: An Umbrella Review." *Health Policy and Planning* 33 (10): 1128–43.

World Bank. 2019. *High-Performance Health Financing for Universal Health Coverage: Driving Sustainable, Inclusive Growth in the 21st Century*. Washington, DC: World Bank.

World Bank. 2022. *Change Cannot Wait: Building Resilient Health Systems in the Shadow of COVID-19*. Washington, DC: World Bank.

World Bank, NIPH (Norwegian Institute of Public Health), and BCEPS (Bergen Centre for Ethics and Priority Setting). 2023. *Open and Inclusive: Fair Processes for Financing Universal Health Coverage*. Washington, DC: World Bank.